FROM THE RED SOX'S REVIVAL TO THE
WORLD BASEBALL CLASSIC, THESE ARE THE
SIGNATURE STORIES THAT DEFINED THE
BEGINNING OF THE 21ST CENTURY.

DECADES

2000–2009

Baseball Insiders Library™

FROM THE RED SOX'S REVIVAL TO THE
WORLD BASEBALL CLASSIC, THESE ARE THE
SIGNATURE STORIES THAT DEFINED THE
BEGINNING OF THE 21ST CENTURY.

DECADES

2000–2009

MLB INSIDERS CLUB

DECADES: 2000–2009 by Jerry Crasnick

From the Red Sox's revival to the World Baseball Classic, these are the signature stories that defined the beginning of the 21st century.

Printed in 2009

ABOUT THE AUTHOR

Jerry Crasnick has covered Major League Baseball for more than two decades for several media outlets. He has written for ESPN.com since 2003, after previously working for the Cincinnati Post, Denver Post *and* Bloomberg News. *In 2005 he released the book* License to Deal: A Season on the Run With a Maverick Baseball Agent. *He lives with his wife and two daughters in Langhorne, Pa.*

ACKNOWLEDGEMENTS

Major League Baseball would like to thank Eric Enders and Kristin Nieto for their diligent work in helping to prepare this book for publication.

MAJOR LEAGUE BASEBALL PROPERTIES

Vice President, Publishing
Donald S. Hintze

Editorial Director
Mike McCormick

Publications Art Director
Faith M. Rittenberg

Senior Production Manager
Claire Walsh

Associate Editor
Jon Schwartz

Associate Art Director
Melanie Finnern

Senior Publishing Coordinator
Anamika Chakrabarty

Project Assistant Editors
Chris Greenberg, Jodie Jordan, Jake Schwartzstein

Editorial Intern
Allison Duffy

MAJOR LEAGUE BASEBALL PHOTOS

Director
Rich Pilling

Photo Editor
Jessica Foster

MLB INSIDERS CLUB

Creative Director
Tom Carpenter

Managing Editor
Jen Weaverling

Prepress
Wendy Holdman

MLB Insiders Club
12301 Whitewater Drive
Minnetonka, MN 55343

TABLE OF CONTENTS

INTRODUCTION

For decades it seemed baseball followed a familiar script, with teams like the Yankees and Cardinals dominating their respective leagues as other clubs, namely the Red Sox, Cubs, White Sox and Phillies, faced torment far too often. But you could pretty much throw the script out the window during the first decade of the 21st century, as surprise after surprise abounded.

Red Sox fans spent more than 80 years lamenting the trade of Babe Ruth, telling Johnny Pesky held-ball stories and rehashing the "Boston Massacre." They suffered through tales of October torment at the hands of Bob Gibson, Bucky Dent and Mookie Wilson. To be sure, the loyal fans of Red Sox Nation were due for a feel-good decade, even if that stretch meant having to endure one last gut-wrenching postseason defeat at the hands of Aaron Boone and the rival Yankees. In 2004, the Sox finally upended New York — in big and bold fashion, coming back from a 3-games-to-none deficit in the ALCS — en route to their first world title since 1918. Just like that, 86 years of emptiness were forgotten.

In 2007, three years after exorcising the "Curse of the Bambino," the Red Sox won it all again, sweeping a young Colorado team that had gone on one of the greatest late-season surges ever, but lost steam during a long wait between the NLCS and the World Series. Boston's two titles set the club apart during a 10-year period that was notable largely for its parity.

The White Sox ended their own 80-plus years without winning a world championship in 2005 behind some colorful personalities, namely candid manager, Ozzie Guillen. On the north side of town, the Cubs passed the century mark since their 1908 World Series victory. And the Phillies ended their city's 25-year sports championship drought when they took home the World Series hardware in 2008. Meanwhile, low-budget teams like the Rockies and Rays — not to mention the Diamondbacks and Astros — all made their first-ever trips to the World Series.

Along the way, the American League continued its domination in the All-Star Game and also excelled in Interleague Play. On the flipside, after dominating the game in the late 1990s, the Yankees beat the Mets for a title in 2000, then fell to Arizona and Florida in the World Series in 2001 and 2003, respectively. Who could have envisioned the Bombers' stretch of early October departures that would ensue?

Some of the most hallowed records in baseball were met and passed during the 2000s. San Francisco's Barry Bonds passed Willie Mays, Babe Ruth and Hank Aaron on the career home run list, and Ichiro Suzuki made history in Seattle a single and a double at a time. Several pitchers joined the 300-win ranks: Greg Maddux, Tom Glavine, Randy Johnson and Roger Clemens.

A parade of franchise faces left the scene during the decade. The Craig Biggio–Jeff Bagwell combination called it quits in Houston; Cal Ripken Jr. and Tony Gwynn were elected to the Hall of Fame; Maddux, Glavine and John Smoltz pitched their last games in Atlanta and played their final round of golf together as Braves after dominating the NL in the previous decade. New ballparks sprung up and talented young players burst onto the scene as MLB set attendance records.

In short, Major League Baseball got turned upside down in the 2000s — and there was nothing wrong with that.

Boston's curse-breaking World Series win in 2004 set the club's tone for the rest of the decade.

CHAPTER I

MOMENTS

Derek Jeter rose to the occasion so many times early in the decade, it was hard to keep track. Do we remember him for his amazing display of instinct on the shovel pass that foiled the A's in the 2001 playoffs, or for his human catapult into the stands to grab a pop fly? The great ones find a way — and sometimes, the good ones do, too. If Dave Roberts gets tagged out in Game 4 of the 2004 ALCS, Boston fans spend another long winter in anguish. But Roberts steals second, and two weeks later the Red Sox are champions. Everything can change in a flash.

BOSTON'S RED SOCK

CURT SCHILLING WON 216 games in the Majors, made six All-Star teams and generated headlines by offering up opinions on various topics regardless of their relation to baseball. Pitching for the Red Sox in the fall of 2004, Schilling made news for his soiled laundry.

Displaying exceptional heart in Game 6 of the American League Championship Series, Schilling pitched seven four-hit innings to beat the Yankees, 4-2. He had injured his right ankle earlier in the playoffs, and he was able to pitch only after Dr. William Morgan, Boston's team physician, devised a procedure to hold a tendon sheath in place with sutures.

The extent of Schilling's injury became clear to millions of television viewers when the cameras zoomed in on his foot and showed blood seeping through his sock. While a few non-believers in the press questioned the veracity of the injury and the discolored sock, the majority of media observers chose to describe Schilling as "courageous" and a "hero."

"I'm proud of that," Schilling said. "It's better than 'bum' and 'idiot,'" the latter being a nickname that the media and fans often used to describe the 2004 squad.

Schilling maintained his winning aura in the World Series, throwing six innings against St. Louis in Boston's 6-2 victory in Game 2. He bloodied another sock, and donated it to the Hall of Fame for a display commemorating Boston's first title in 86 years. Schilling's sock, a Manny Ramirez bat and several other items told the story of Boston's World Series sweep.

FACE PLANT

PHILADELPHIA FANS CAN be notoriously tough on their local sports personalities, but it didn't take them long to develop a soft spot for Phillies outfielder Aaron Rowand. After all,

Schilling pitched Game 6 of the 2004 ALCS against the Yankees with a severely injured ankle. His bloody sock became the symbol of his performance.

how could fans not love a ballplayer who leaves an imprint of his face on the outfield wall in pursuit of a fly ball?

Rowand, who came to Philadelphia from Chicago in November 2005, quickly earned a reputation for selfless play. His signature moment came on May 11, 2006, when he chased down a drive by the Mets' Xavier Nady at the warning track, caught the ball and crashed into an unpadded metal bar, suffering a broken nose and opening a gash that required 15 stitches to close. Other than that, he pronounced himself fine after the collision.

"I wasn't all that pretty to begin with," he said.

The locals quickly showed their appreciation. Sales of Aaron Rowand T-shirts spiked in the Phillies' gift shop after the catch, and Rowand received a standing ovation upon his return from the disabled list. A Vietnam veteran wrote a letter to the Philadelphia *Daily News* with the headline, "Aaron Rowand's the kind of guy you want in your foxhole."

Even fans in opposing parks shouted out to Rowand during pregame stretching to tell him how much they appreciated his effort.

"It's overwhelming," Rowand said. "You can't compliment me any better than that."

VERLANDER SOARS

BIG LEAGUE PLAYERS are used to explaining away gaffes by attributing them to the sun getting in their eyes or losing the ball in the lights. Fans and reporters have grown accustomed to such clichés. After striking out four times in a game against Detroit, Milwaukee infielder Tony Graffanino gave a truly original excuse for whiff No. 1.

"I actually swung at a bird," Graffanino said of his first-inning strikeout.

The incredible game Detroit fans saw on July 12, 2007, included a fowl subplot. In late spring 2007, storms carried moths from the southern states to Michigan. The moths were

This page: Rowand crashes into the outfield wall during a 2006 game against the rival Mets. Opposite: The Detroit Tigers swarm Verlander following his 2007 no-hitter.

attracted to the lights at Comerica Park, and seagulls arrived on the scene to feast. As the birds fluttered around the infield, they made for a surreal backdrop to a masterful performance by the Tigers' Justin Verlander and provided a handy excuse for Graffanino.

Even with the birds, Verlander's triple-digit fastball generated most of the conversation after he struck out 12 batters in a 4-0, no-hit win over the Brewers. Verlander opened the game by retiring the first seven batters — three on strikeouts — before issuing his first walk. Typical with most no-hitters, Verlander had some help from his fielders, including a sliding catch from Magglio Ordonez in the seventh inning on a sinking line drive.

Once the game ended on a 101-mph heater and the no-hitter was in the books, TV cameras captured Tigers Hall of Famer Al Kaline applauding from the press box in appreciation. It was clear that Verlander had just soared to new heights.

FOR THE BIRDS

Thanks to some ingenuity from the Tigers' staff, the infestation of seagulls that swarmed Detroit's Comerica Park in various games during the 2007 season didn't last all year. Tigers head groundskeeper Heather Nabozny consulted with area golf courses, and they recommended the use of dogs to disperse the birds. So the Tigers brought in a pair of black Labrador retrievers and supplemented them with plastic owls placed strategically around the field.

Before long, Comerica Park's gull problem was history, and visiting hitters could concentrate on trying to catch up with the likes of Justin Verlander's heat instead of coping with winged intruders. Verlander finished the season with an 18-6 record, so apparently he didn't need much outside help.

BUGGED DOWN

Down, 1-0, to New York in Game 2 of the 2007 American League Division Series, and with Joba Chamberlain and Mariano Rivera lined up and ready to deal in the Yankees' bullpen, the Cleveland Indians were reduced to praying for a sudden rainstorm or a miracle. Perhaps a plague of locusts.

They got neither rain nor divine intervention. But Option C certainly came close.

In one of the most bizarre natural occurrences in baseball history, the Indians rallied to beat New York, 2-1, when Chamberlain, the Yankees' hard-throwing rookie set-up man, was distracted by a swarm of flying insects known as midges coming in from nearby Lake Erie.

Cleveland scratched out a run off a suddenly wild Chamberlain in the eighth, and won it, 2-1, when Travis Hafner singled home Kenny Lofton in the 11th. It was the first time anyone could recall a pitcher twice summoning the training staff from the dugout to shower him with bug spray.

"Just when you think you've seen it all, you see something new," Yankees shortstop Derek Jeter said. "I guess that's the home-field advantage for them — just let the bugs out in the eighth inning. It worked."

In contrast to Chamberlain, Indians starter Fausto Carmona maintained his focus throughout the buggy infestation in the top of the ninth inning.

"It just shows what kind of guy he is," said teammate Ryan Garko. "It doesn't matter if it's raining, it's hot, it's cold or there are bugs. He just goes out there and pitches his heart out."

JOBA CHAMBERLAIN'S 2007 STATS								
REGULAR SEASON								
ERA	IP	W-L	BB	K	SV	K/BB	WHIP	
0.38	24.0	2-0	6	34	1	5.67	0.75	
ALDS								
ERA	IP	W-L	BB	K	SV	K/BB	WHIP	
4.91	3.2	0-0	3	4	0	1.33	1.64	

IN THE LINE OF FIRE

IN DECEMBER 2002, as baseball's general managers talked trades at their annual offseason meetings, they also pushed for a provision requiring batboys to be at least 14 years of age. The initiative, which was passed shortly thereafter, became known as the "The Darren Baker rule."

Little Darren, the son of San Francisco Manager Dusty Baker, was 3-and-a-half years old in October 2002 when the Giants reached the World Series. He was a beloved presence in the clubhouse, the team's resident good luck charm and a symbol of his father's efforts to turn the game into a family affair. Several sons of players rotated in and out of the dugout as team batboys during the season.

But Darren's enthusiasm got the better of him during San Francisco's 16-4 win over the Angels in Game 5 of the Fall Classic. After Giants outfielder Kenny Lofton lashed a triple off the wall, Darren sprinted from the dugout to retrieve the bat and was camped too close to the plate for comfort.

J.T. Snow, who had been standing on third base, crossed home plate on Lofton's hit, alertly scooped up Darren by his jacket collar, and carried him to safety before the littlest Giant could be steamrolled by incoming baserunner David Bell.

"His eyes were huge," Snow said. "I don't think he knew what was going on."

Dusty Baker later received a stern lecture from his mother, Christina, who was upset about seeing her grandson in harm's way. Darren, properly chastened, was allowed to travel with the Giants to Anaheim for Game 6. As for Snow, he was proclaimed a hero for his quick thinking and alert reactions.

"I might get on the highlights for once by saving Dusty's kid," Snow said.

THE FLIP

DEREK JETER BUILT a Hall-of-Fame reputation in New York with a fundamentally sound approach both at the plate and in the field, and a knack for being in the right spot at the right time. On perhaps the most memorable play of his career, Jeter's instincts took him to a place on the field that only he could have imagined.

Previous spread: Manager Joe Torre meets with Chamberlain and Yankees infielders amidst a swarm of midges in Cleveland during the 2007 ALDS. Opposite: Snow rescues young Baker from a near collision at the plate during Game 5 of the 2002 World Series.

Trailing, 2 games to none, in the 2001 Division Series, the Yankees were leading Oakland, 1-0, in Game 3 when trouble began for New York pitcher Mike Mussina. Jeremy Giambi singled, and Terrence Long followed with a shot inside the first-base bag. Right fielder Shane Spencer retrieved the ball, but his throw home sailed over cutoff man Alfonso Soriano and backup cutoff man Tino Martinez, and the ball bounced toward no man's land in the infield, along the first-base line.

Enter Jeter, who appeared out of nowhere to flag down the throw, then flipped a backhand lateral to Jorge Posada. The Yankees' catcher tagged out Giambi as he inexplicably failed to slide.

"I didn't have time to turn around, set up and throw," Jeter said later. "Basically, I just got rid of it. If I tried to spin around, he would have been safe."

The Yankees hung on for a 1-0 victory, and won the next two games to take the series. Jeter hit .444 (8 for 18), and made another memorable play in Game 5 when he crashed into the stands to catch a long foul ball.

"I've never seen an athlete dominate any sport — in baseball, in basketball, in football — like he dominated this series," said Yankees Owner George Steinbrenner of Jeter.

MELTDOWN

When a franchise is on its way to a century of championship futility, no one is immune from the crossfire — not even a 26-year-old diehard fan just looking for a souvenir. Steve Bartman, a lifelong Cubs backer and local youth baseball coach, was rooting for the team from his seat at Wrigley Field in the 2003 National League Championship Series against Florida when he was unwittingly thrust into the action.

With Chicago leading, 3-0, and five outs from its first World Series appearance since 1945, the Marlins' Luis Castillo lofted a foul pop to left. Cubs left fielder Moises Alou reached into the stands to catch the ball, but Bartman — along with several other fans — reached for it, as well. The ball hit off Bartman's hands and deflected away.

Alou threw down his glove in disgust as Cubs fans booed. Still, Chicago had a three-run lead with team ace Mark Prior on the mound. The North Siders were still in control of the game. But the right-hander followed by walking Castillo, and Ivan Rodriguez subsequently hit an RBI single to left field to cut the deficit to two. Prior seemingly got out of the jam when the next batter, Miguel Cabrera, hit a routine double-play ball to shortstop Alex Gonzalez, who led all NL shortstops that year in fielding percentage. Gonzalez booted the ball, though, loading the bases. On the next pitch, Derrek Lee lined a two-run double to left field to tie the game. The Cubs' bullpen took over from there, but couldn't stop the bleeding, as the Marlins ultimately scored eight runs in the inning.

During this collapse, Bartman suffered from catcalls and flying objects, and had to be escorted from his seat by security guards to ensure his safety. Even though the Cubs' players were ultimately responsible for the Game 6 loss and eventual Series defeat, Bartman issued a written apology the next day to Alou, Cubs fans, franchise icons Ron Santo and Ernie Banks and the entire Cubs organization.

"I am so truly sorry from the bottom of this Cub fan's broken heart," Bartman said.

Although the disappointment lingered, the tangible evidence eventually disintegrated. The "Bartman ball" sold for $113,824 at an auction, and it was later blown up by a Hollywood special effects expert in a ceremony at Harry Caray's restaurant in Chicago.

THE STEAL

Dave Roberts became aware of his place in Boston sports history when he attended a football game at his alma mater, UCLA, and a member of Red Sox Nation came up to thank him in the stadium restroom.

"The guy was looking over — at my eyes — and said, 'Hey, I'm a Red Sox fan. Thank you for the stolen base,'" Roberts said. "That one takes the cake."

The Red Sox have historically valued power over speed, but Roberts made his mark with his wheels in October 2004. His stolen base against the Yankees in Game 4 of the American League Championship Series fueled a Red Sox comeback from a 3-games-to-none deficit, and made him a hero in the eyes of the team's fans.

With the Red Sox trailing, 4-3, in the ninth inning, Yankees closer Mariano Rivera walked leadoff hitter Kevin Millar, and Boston sent Roberts in to pinch-run.

The Cubs' collapse in the 2003 NLCS against the Marlins has often been disproportionately blamed on a fan who reached out and deflected a Marlins' foul pop-up that Chicago outfielder Alou had been attempting to reel in.

The speedy outfielder had done his homework. He studied game tape and knew that Rivera would try to disrupt his rhythm by holding the ball before delivering each pitch. After Rivera threw over to first three times, Roberts took off for second and barely beat a strong throw from catcher Jorge Posada.

"Once I got my jump, I had a good feeling I was going to be safe," Roberts said later. "But when I looked back at the videotape, I didn't realize how close it was. I thought I was in there for sure. Then I looked at the videotape and it was a very surreal moment. It was bang-bang."

Roberts then scored on Bill Mueller's base hit to begin the comeback that kick-started Boston's run to a championship. Roberts, in hindsight, was aware of the risks inherent in trying to steal second at such a critical spot. He knew exactly what was at stake.

"It was my first time in the ALCS and an opportunity for me to do something special," Roberts said. "There were a lot of emotions going through my head, like: 'If I get thrown out, I'm going to be the next Billy Buckner. But if I do make it, then something positive could happen and there could be a turning of the tide.'"

BELLY FLOP

PHILADELPHIA PHILLIES SHORTSTOP Jimmy Rollins may have walked away with the 2007 National League Most Valuable Player Award. But Colorado Rockies outfielder Matt Holliday, his main rival for the award, produced the regular-season exclamation point to remember.

Holliday, breaking through as a star at age 27, led the National League with a .340 batting average and 137 RBI. He also ranked first in the league in hits, total bases and doubles. But Holliday's signature moment didn't come until the 163rd game of the season, when he sacrificed his chin to lead the Rockies past the Padres and into the postseason.

Holliday's Rockies won 13 of their last 14 regular-season games to force a one-game playoff with San Diego. After allowing the Padres to tie the contest in the eighth inning, it appeared the Rockies had lost the momentum heading into extra frames. Then in the 13th, San Diego plated two runs on a Scott Hairston homer. With future Hall of Famer Trevor Hoffman coming out of the bullpen for the Padres, it seemed the Rockies' run would be stopped short. But Colorado never lost faith, scoring three times in the bottom of the inning to post a stunning 9-8 victory.

Colorado's winning rally consisted of doubles by Kaz Matsui and Troy Tulowitzki, a Holliday triple, a walk and a Jamey Carroll sacrifice fly. Holliday beat the throw from right fielder Brian Giles, and umpire Tim McClelland signaled safe even though the replays cast some doubt on whether Holliday touched home plate with his left hand.

During Holliday's belly flop–like slide, he gashed his chin. He felt the sting from the champagne during the post-game celebration, but no one heard him complain.

"I've seen this on TV a lot and I'm excited to be part of it," Holliday said. "I've always wanted to spray whatever that stuff is all over the place."

SMALL BALL

THE PARTICIPANTS IN the final Yankee Stadium All-Star Game were so intent on making the occasion memorable, it appeared they might play forever.

The 2008 Midsummer Classic lasted for 15 innings — at four hours and 50 minutes, the longest All-Star Game ever. The managers, Terry Francona of the AL and Clint Hurdle of the NL, exhausted their benches, nearly ran out of pitchers and actually entertained

Opposite: Roberts steals second in the ninth inning during Game 4 of the 2004 ALCS and keeps Boston's championship dream alive. Next spread: Holliday dives home with the winning run to clinch the 2007 NL Wild Card.

the possibility of Mets third baseman David Wright pitching for the NL and Boston right fielder J.D. Drew dusting off his mound assortment for the AL.

Mercifully, it never came to that. Texas's Michael Young lofted a sacrifice fly to right field to score Justin Morneau with the game-winner in the bottom of the 15th, and the American League extended its undefeated All-Star Game streak to 12 with a 4-3 victory.

The marathon running time was appropriate given that the National League received a pregame pep talk from Hall of Famer Ernie Banks, whose signature motto was "Let's play two!" The two sides nearly made Mr. Cub's slogan a reality.

"Yankee Stadium is tough, I'm telling you," said New York closer Mariano Rivera, who pitched 1.2 innings amid flashing camera bulbs and an appreciative crowd offering its respects in the Bronx. "She didn't want the game to end. But she finally gave it up for us. She was tough."

By the time the game ended at 1:37 a.m., many of the participants were too drained to put it into words. But not Young.

"It just shows how this game is special," Young said. "Football has a game after the season. In hockey they can't go full-blast into each other. Basketball is an alley-oop fest. Not baseball."

LATE NIGHT IN THE BRONX

What do you do during a 15-inning All-Star Game? If you're Brad Lidge, you throw approximately 100 pitches during six stretches in the bullpen before coming out for your one inning of work. And if you're Derek Jeter, a de facto host of the 2008 Midsummer Classic, you spend most of the time watching.

After being removed from the game, the Yankees' captain stuck around, nearly as transfixed as the millions of fans who couldn't turn away. "It seemed like the stadium didn't want it to end," Jeter said inside the victorious AL clubhouse. Jeter's classy gesture wasn't the only one of the night. In fact, Jeter was the beneficiary of a respectful move by AL skipper Terry Francona. Although the Red Sox and Yankees are rivals, Francona heaped plenty of tributes upon New York players — he used Mariano Rivera as his ninth-inning man, and removed both Jeter and Alex Rodriguez in the middle of innings to allow them each an additional ovation.

RUNNING OUT OF STEAM

Dɪᴅ Bᴏsᴛᴏɴ ᴍᴀɴᴀɢᴇʀ Grady Little make the wrong decision or simply fall victim to bad luck and worse karma? Regardless of his explanation, Red Sox fans weren't in much of a mood to forgive following Boston's exit from the 2003 playoffs.

The Red Sox, on the verge of closing out the Yankees in Game 7 of the 2003 American League Championship Series, sent three-time Cy Young winner Pedro Martinez to the

mound with a 5-2 lead in the bottom of the eighth inning. Martinez had struck out eight batters in his first seven frames of work while issuing just one walk. Just two more innings, and the American League pennant would be theirs. But it was not to be. New York rallied against a weary Martinez, pulling within two on a Derek Jeter double, a Bernie Williams single and a Hideki Matsui ground-rule double. Fans all over New England suspected Martinez was cooked. Everyone seemed to know that he had emptied his tank except for two people: Martinez and the man going to the mound to check on the Boston ace.

Upon making a mound visit to check with Martinez on his condition, Little didn't take the ball from his best pitcher, and it cost him. Jorge Posada delivered a bloop double to tie the game and send Yankee Stadium into a frenzy. Three tense, scoreless innings later, Aaron Boone's home run off Tim Wakefield gave New York a 6-5 victory — and the Series. The Bronx erupted in jubilation, Yankees closer Mariano Rivera stormed out of the dugout and collapsed on the mound, and Red Sox Nation was faced with another winter of "what if's."

Several days later at Fenway Park, Little defended his decision to stick with Martinez for 123 pitches.

"If people want to judge Grady Little on the results of a decision I made in that last game the other day, so be it," Little said. "In my heart, I know we had a great season here."

Not great enough to save his job. Shortly thereafter, the Red Sox declined to exercise Little's contract option despite his team's 188-136 record over two seasons.

BASEBALL'S HEALING POWER

As COMMISSIONER BUD Selig tried to decide when the games should resume after the terrorist attacks of Sept. 11, 2001, he was reminded that baseball can play a helpful role in the healing process after a national trauma.

There was no greater evidence than the first game back in New York, just a few miles from the tragic events at Ground Zero. The city was still in a state of shock as a crowd of 41,235 gathered at Shea Stadium on Sept. 21 to watch the Mets play the Braves. Mayor Rudy Giuliani and entertainers Liza Minnelli and Diana Ross took part in the pregame ceremonies, and the New York players looked on solemnly with the date of the tragedy — 9-11-01 — sewn onto their uniform sleeves.

All-Star catcher Mike Piazza, who grew up near Philadelphia but had come to embrace New York during his four seasons as a Met, seemed especially touched by the events. Piazza fought back tears before the game as police officers and firefighters honored their fallen brothers and sisters. Mets players wore caps that were emblazoned with the logos of various city agencies that were involved in the recovery efforts.

"I remember standing on the line during the national anthem — actually when the bagpipes and band came out — and I said to myself, 'Please God, give me the strength to get through this,'" Piazza later said.

Piazza did his part late in the game with an at-bat that shook the stadium and momentarily lifted the spirits of the Big Apple. With his team trailing, 2-1, in the bottom of the eighth against the rival Braves, he hit a two-run homer off Atlanta reliever Steve Karsay to give the Mets a 3-2 lead. The crowd rose en masse and felt a wave of exhilaration that emanated through the TV airwaves.

Said Atlanta pitcher Tom Glavine, "I was kind of getting that feeling of, 'Well, this is one of those nights where maybe there's a higher authority that's watching over this. Maybe this is happening for a much bigger reason.'"

Opposite: Morneau crosses the plate just before Brian McCann can apply the tag, ending the 2008 All-Star Game in the 15th inning. Next spread: Manager Bobby Valentine and Piazza during ceremonies before the Mets resume play on Sept. 21, 2001.

23

CHAPTER 2

RECORDS

Barry Bonds' 756th homer was the biggest record-breaking news of the decade, but top dogs can find ways to make history without clearing the fence. Craig Biggio set a record for collecting the most black-and-blue marks, and Ichiro Suzuki did it one line drive at a time. Carl Crawford dazzled the Red Sox with his wheels, and Omar Vizquel stood apart just by showing up. We saw cycles and hitting streaks, and a relay team-and-a-half of Astros pitchers shut down the Yankees in the Bronx. We even saw a 30-run game during a long day in Baltimore. Imagine that …

HOMETOWN LOVE

AT THE BEGINNING of the 2009 season, Chavez Ravine seemed as giddy as it was when Kirk Gibson pumped his fist circling first base on one leg in the 1988 World Series, or during the height of Fernandomania. Through the first two homestands of the '09 campaign, the Los Angeles Dodgers won blowouts and squeakers, pitching duels and shootouts. While the scripts varied, the ending was always the same — smiles, back slaps and high fives exchanged by Dodgers players in the field.

Dodgers fans expected big things in Joe Torre's second year as the manager, and the club's hot start did nothing to temper the optimism. Los Angeles won its first 13 games at Dodger Stadium to break the record for home wins to begin a season, held previously by the 1911 Detroit Tigers, who were led by Hall of Famers Ty Cobb and Sam Crawford.

The Dodgers celebrated their accomplishment with a catered steak dinner, but Torre seemed more relieved than jubilant after his team broke open a close game to beat the Washington Nationals, 10-3, for the record.

"Streaks are fine, but we have more important things in mind," Torre said. "Hopefully, it's just a stepping stone on the way to something more important."

The Dodgers' rotation gave unexpectedly strong performances during the winning streak, and plenty of offense was generated around marquee slugger Manny Ramirez. But as General Manager Ned Colletti pointedly reminded reporters: "It's a baseball season. It's not a baseball month."

If only May were as serene as April. The day after the Dodgers notched win No. 13, they lost Ramirez to a 50-game suspension. As if on cue, the Dodgers blew a lead to Washington and lost, 11-9. The defeat ended the streak, but couldn't touch the team's momentum.

The Dodgers celebrate after beating the Padres at Dodger Stadium on May 3, 2009, for their 10th straight home win.

27

SLICK SHORTSTOP

IF THE MARK of a man is the company he keeps, then Omar Vizquel should have a compelling case for the Hall of Fame. Vizquel, an 11-time Gold Glove Award winner at shortstop, set two records in the span of a little more than a year that will serve as a testament over time to his sustained brilliance. In May of 2007, Vizquel turned the 1,591st double play of his career to break the record he shared with Ozzie Smith. The following May, Vizquel played in his 2,584th game at shortstop to break the record held by Luis Aparicio.

Vizquel, all 5-foot-9 and 165 pounds of him, is part of a proud and accomplished line of standout shortstops from Venezuela. The list includes Aparicio, Chico Carrasquel, Dave Concepcion and Ozzie Guillen, as well as Alex Gonzalez, Cesar Izturis and Elvis Andrus in more recent years.

Vizquel, undersized and not blessed with an especially strong throwing arm, relied on soft hands, quick feet and exceptional range to make his mark in the field throughout his career. He displayed an uncanny knack for going back into the outfield to catch pop flies, and routinely put on a show around the bag during infield practice.

The ultimate reward for Vizquel's record-breaking tendencies came when Aparicio showed up at the press conference honoring Vizquel for his 2,584th game at shortstop.

"I'm fortunate," Vizquel said. "I'm lucky that God gave me health and kept me healthy throughout my career. Like Luis said, it's not easy to play a demanding position like shortstop."

END OF TWO ERAS

FITTINGLY ENOUGH, IN a decade that possessed no shortage of competitive balance, two of Major League Baseball's most dominant franchises finally discovered how it feels to finish an entire season without experiencing a single champagne celebration.

The Atlanta Braves had won a division title for an unprecedented 14 straight years, not counting the strike-shortened 1994 season. But Atlanta's streak ended in 2006, when bullpen problems and a 19-33 record in one-run games left the team with just 79 wins and a third-place finish in the National League East.

This page: Jones was an integral piece of the Braves' dynasty. Opposite: The agile Vizquel broke Smith's double-play record in May 2007.

The Braves won just a single world championship during their postseason run, and while many believe that the World Series hardware ultimately signifies success, General Manager John Schuerholz — the architect of those excellent teams — believed that observers failed to grasp the magnitude of the club's achievements.

"I think this streak will look more grand and will stand more strongly at its end than it was appreciated in the middle," he said.

The New York Yankees, similarly, had grown accustomed to playing in October. Starting with the 1995 club, which made the playoffs as a Wild Card under Manager Buck Showalter, the Yankees made the playoffs 13 seasons in a row before falling short in 2008.

"It basically just boils down to we weren't good enough," said shortstop Derek Jeter, who appeared in the postseason with the Yankees every year from 1996 to 2007. "Our team didn't play well enough the whole season in order to get to where we needed to be. It's a huge disappointment."

EN FUEGO

JIMMY ROLLINS AND Chase Utley — double-play partners, fellow All-Stars and world champion celebrants in Philadelphia — shared another novel distinction in the 2000s: They became the first set of teammates to lead the league in hitting streaks in consecutive years since Willie Mays (20 games in 1963) and Willie McCovey (24 in 1964) with the Giants.

Rollins, Philadelphia's shortstop, hit safely in 36 straight games to end the 2005 campaign, and then began '06 with hits in the first two games. His streak ended at 38 when he went 0 for 4 against St. Louis on April 6, 2006. Just a few months later, Utley, the Phillies' second baseman, delivered a knock in 35 straight games before going 0 for 5 in a game against the Mets at Shea Stadium on Aug. 4, 2006.

Along with showcasing the respective talents of the two players, the streaks highlighted the differences in their personalities. Rollins, energetic and outgoing, had fun with his streak and seemed to enjoy the daily banter with reporters. Utley, quiet and businesslike, habitually steered pre- and post-game conversation away from his streak. When Philadelphia beat writers mentioned it in interviews, Utley often changed the subject and discussed his teammates' performances or even the weather. Utley even refrained from discussing the topic with fellow Phillies for fear of jinxing himself.

"He might be superstitious or whatever. But me, I didn't care," Rollins said. "I didn't have any idea where I was. I knew I had a lot of consecutive games, but I didn't know what the number was. That's just my personality."

The Utley and Rollins streaks came several years after another NL East middle infielder made a splash with his hitting acumen. Florida second baseman Luis Castillo hit safely in 35 straight games in 2002 before taking an 0-fer in an Interleague game against Detroit. Castillo's streak was the longest since the Milwaukee Brewers' Paul Molitor put together a 39-game run in 1987.

HIT MACHINE

AT 5-FOOT-9 AND 160 pounds, Seattle Mariners outfielder Ichiro Suzuki lacks the dominant physical presence typically associated with an offensive powerhouse. But his lithe physique belies a serious appetite for base hits. Ichiro recorded 242, 208 and 212 hits in his first three seasons as a Mariner before taking his production to a new level in 2004, when he accumulated a staggering 262 hits to break the record of 257, which was held by George Sisler of the 1920 St. Louis Browns.

Rollins hit in 38 straight games for the Phillies, a streak that spanned two seasons from 2005–06.

Ichiro topped Sisler in Seattle's 160th regular-season game, against Texas pitcher Ryan Drese. He chopped a single over the glove of Rangers third baseman Hank Blalock in the first inning, then lined a base hit past the dive of Texas shortstop Michael Young in the third for base knock No. 258.

The sellout crowd of 45,573 at Safeco Field rejoiced to the accompaniment of fireworks and the theme song from the movie *The Natural*. Ichiro's fellow Mariners streamed out of the dugout to offer their congratulations, and he took time out to walk over to the stands and greet the five members of the Sisler family who were in attendance.

"It's definitely the most emotional I have gotten in my life," Ichiro said. "It's definitely the highlight of my career, and I was thinking, 'Is there something better in my future?'"

As Ichiro continued to pile up 200-hit seasons, All-Star Game appearances and World Baseball Classic titles through the end of the decade, the answer to that question was self-evident.

POWER RANGERS

THE TEXAS RANGERS set a franchise record for runs scored in a doubleheader on Aug. 22, 2007, at Camden Yards in Baltimore. Then the second game got under way.

Just hours after the Orioles held a press conference to announce that Interim Manager Dave Trembley would return for the 2008 season, the Rangers took a crowbar to the festivities. They routed the Orioles, 30-3, in the opener to become the first team in the modern era to score 30 runs in a game. The Rangers became the first team to reach the 30-run mark since the 1897 Chicago Colts, who later became the Cubs, beat the Louisville Colonels, 36-7. Texas took it relatively easy on the Orioles in the second game, winning by a mere two runs, 9-7.

"The one thing you hope is they have blisters from the first game," said Baltimore's Kevin Millar. "I've never seen 30. Thank God they don't get two wins for the one game."

Every player in the Texas starting lineup contributed at least two hits, and Jarrod Salta-lamacchia and Ramon Vazquez combined to go 8 for 12 with four home runs and 14 RBI out of the bottom two spots in the batting order. Incredibly, entering the sixth inning the Rangers only led, 5-3, before going wild against the Baltimore bullpen.

"This is something freaky," said Texas outfielder Marlon Byrd, who hit a grand slam in the sixth. "You won't see anything like this again for a long, long time."

TEAM EFFORT

ONE MINUTE BRAD Lidge was taking in Monument Park with a sense of exhilaration and wonder, just like so many do when they set foot in Yankee Stadium for the first time. And just a few hours later, he was drinking champagne inside the visiting clubhouse with his bullpen buddies, celebrating the fact that he had combined with five other Houston pitchers to throw a no-hitter in an 8-0 Astros victory over New York.

"We thought George Steinbrenner sent [the champagne] over," Lidge said. "Then somebody asked him about it and he said, 'Are you crazy? I'd never do that.'"

In the long, tradition-laden history of Yankee Stadium, the events of June 11, 2003, have to qualify among the most surreal. Astros starter Roy Oswalt lasted just 21 pitches before being forced to leave the game in the bottom of the second inning with a groin strain. His manager, Jimy Williams, figured it would be a long night as he signaled for reliever Pete Munro.

But while the relievers kept on coming for Houston, the hits never did for New York. Munro, Kirk Saarloos, Lidge, Octavio Dotel and Billy Wagner stifled the Yankees for

Opposite: Ichiro broke Sisler's single-season hits mark. This page: Six Astros pitchers held the Yankees hitless.

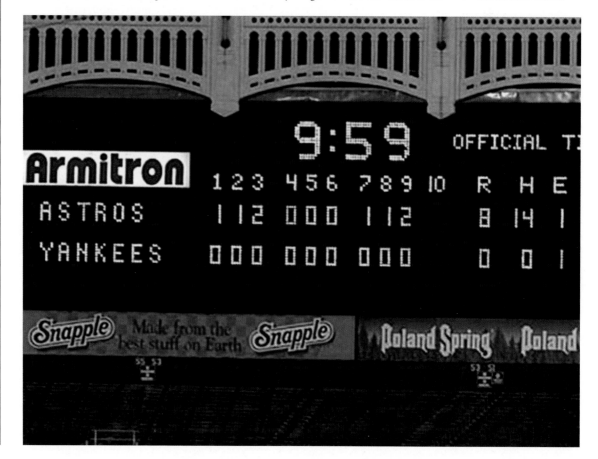

eight additional innings, with Wagner retiring Hideki Matsui on a groundout to conclude the first no-hitter against New York since Baltimore's Hoyt Wilhelm spun one in 1958.

Before Houston's relay combination, the record for the number of pitchers used during a no-hitter was four. Vida Blue and the Oakland A's bullpen tossed a gem against the California Angels in

SIX ASTROS PITCHERS THROW NO-HITTER

	IP	H	BB	K
Roy Oswalt	1.0	0	0	2
Pete Munro	2.2	0	3	2
Kirk Saarloos	1.1	0	0	1
Brad Lidge	2.0	0	0	2
Octavio Dotel	1.0	0	0	4
Billy Wagner	1.0	0	0	2

September of 1975, and in 1991, Baltimore's Bob Milacki combined with three Orioles relievers to achieve the feat against Oakland.

"First appearance for most of us in Yankee Stadium," Wagner said. "What better place could there be?"

Yankees Manager Joe Torre, understandably, did not share Wagner's enthusiasm.

"This is one of the worst games I've ever been involved in," Torre said. "It was a total, inexcusable performance."

THE FLASH

TAMPA BAY OUTFIELDER Carl Crawford earned a reputation as a triples machine during his first seven campaigns in the Big Leagues, particularly from the 2004 season through 2008, when he banged out 69 three-baggers to rank first in the Majors in that category.

As the Boston Red Sox discovered early in the 2009 season, Crawford also has a flair for getting to third base in increments.

The left fielder reached base five times during a 5-3 victory over Boston on May 3 and spent his day tormenting catcher Jason Varitek and the Boston pitching staff. Crawford joined Eddie Collins, Otis Nixon and Eric Young as the only post-1900 players to steal six bases in a game.

Tampa Bay's Michel Hernandez and Jason Bartlett joined in the fun, and the go-go Rays became the first American League team in 11 years to steal eight bases in a game.

Crawford's onslaught was even more impressive considering he was oblivious to the record. He told reporters he would have tried to steal a seventh bag if he had known history was within his reach.

The Rays and Tropicana Field acknowledged Crawford's achievement with a message on the outfield scoreboard, to which the crowd of 32,332 fans roared in appreciation. "Oh, that's what they were cheering about," Crawford said. "I thought they were just cheering. I didn't look. I was paying attention to the game."

Stolen bases came back into vogue during the 2009 season thanks to Crawford and some other speedsters like fellow Ray B.J. Upton and Boston's Jacoby Ellsbury. The Colorado Rockies' quick outfielder Dexter Fowler set a modern rookie record with five steals against San Diego on April 27.

MAN OF STEEL

CRAIG BIGGIO SHOWED baseball fans in Houston the true meaning of self-sacrifice by shifting from catcher to second base to the outfield during his two decades as an Astro. He finished his career with 3,060 career hits, 1,844 runs scored, seven All-Star Game appearances and five Silver Slugger Awards.

The Rays' Crawford steals his second of six bases against the Red Sox on May 3, 2009.

But Biggio truly showed his willingness to put his team ahead of himself through his capacity for collecting a type of mark most often left out of the record books: welts and bruises.

The Houston star made history on June 29, 2005, when he was hit by a pitch for the 268th time to break Don Baylor's modern-day record. Colorado's Byung-Hyun Kim did the honors, clipping the black protective pad that Biggio wore to shield his left elbow. The pad eventually made it to the Hall of Fame in Cooperstown, N.Y.

He went on to conclude his career with 285 HBP's, two short of the all-time mark held by Hughie Jennings, who began his career with the Louisville Colonels in 1891. But Biggio is the guy who will long be remembered for setting baseball's standard for courage — or bull-headedness — in the face of danger.

During his career, Biggio was drilled by a slew of Major League hurlers, including two pairs of brother acts — Alan and Andy Benes and Al and Mark Leiter — as well as Cy Young Award winners Greg Maddux, Roger Clemens and Pedro Martinez. His most painful season came in 1997, when he was plunked a whopping 34 times.

"Maybe there is a part of the brain that I don't have that says, 'Get out of the way,'" Biggio said jokingly.

HIT MAN

Few players would mind being awarded the superlative, "Most willing to take one for the team." But in that vein, there also must be a pitcher who has hit the most batters in his career.

That honor goes to Hall of Famer Walter Johnson, who played for the Washington Senators from 1907–27. Throughout his playing days, Johnson hit a total of 203 batters to set the record. Although he hit an average of just 10 batters a year, his career spanned 21 seasons.

Hitting the greatest number of batters isn't Johnson's only historical claim to fame. Nicknamed "The Big Train," he was one of baseball's early greats, amassing 417 career wins and a 2.17 career ERA. The two-time American League MVP compiled a dozen 20-plus win seasons, and his strikeout record of 3,509 K's stood for 55 years until it was shattered by Nolan Ryan in 1983.

Of pitchers who threw in the 2000s, Randy Johnson hit the most batters, including a career high 18 in 1992 and 2001.

IN MEMORY ...

AFTER TEXAS SECOND baseman Ian Kinsler went 6 for 6 and hit for the cycle on April 15, 2009, his fellow Rangers, the Baltimore Orioles, baseball fans in Arlington and assorted media members were left to ponder the following question: Which was more impressive — his hitting or his timing?

Kinsler became the first player to go 6 for 6 with a single, a double, a triple and a home run in a nine-inning game since William (Farmer) Weaver achieved the feat for the 1890 Louisville Colonels against the Syracuse Stars. Before Kinsler's history-making day against the Orioles, Bobby Veach of the 1920 Detroit Tigers and Rondell White of the 1995 Montreal Expos had notched six-hit cycles in extra-inning games. Kinsler joined Mark Teixeira, Oddibe McDowell and Gary Matthews Jr. on the list of Rangers to complete the cycle.

Coincidentally, Kinsler happened to go wild on a day honoring one of the elite second basemen in Major League history.

"It is more special to do it on Jackie Robinson Day," Kinsler said. "He's the guy who could do everything in the game — hit triples, hit home runs, steal bases, score runs, do everything. It is weird that it's Jackie Robinson Day and I'm playing second base, but it's great it happened that way."

Kinsler, who joined the Major Leagues as a 17th-round draft pick, has shown the ability to do a lot in this game, too. A year prior to his historical offensive day, he was a serious contender for the AL MVP Award before suffering a season-ending sports hernia in mid-August.

Opposite: Biggio is hit for the 268th time on June 29, 2005. Next spread: Kinsler celebrates a solo home run on April 15, 2009, part of his 6-for-6 day that included a cycle.

CHAPTER 3
BALLPARKS

Baseball's latest stadium construction craze began in earnest in the 1990s, with Baltimore's Camden Yards setting the standard for modern interpretations of old-time charm. The 2000s brought new parks, with brick exteriors, jumbo scoreboards and quirky designs, not to mention cheese steaks in Philadelphia, garlic fries in San Francisco and grilled kosher dogs in Milwaukee. Fans loved the wide concourses and superior views, players liked jumping off the bench without conking their heads on dugout roofs, and the sterile concrete bowls of the '70s became a memory.

THE HEARTLAND

ST. LOUIS MANAGER Tony La Russa has never been much for sentiment. He's so engrossed in winning games that he rarely takes time to stop and smell the roses — never mind the popcorn, the hot dogs or the freshly cut grass.

But Opening Day at the new Busch Stadium in April 2006 was too blissful to ignore. The sky was a cloudless blue and the temperature hovered near 70 degrees. The majestic Budweiser Clydesdales circled the field to the accompaniment of the Budweiser theme song, which heralded the arrival of Stan Musial, Red Schoendienst, Bob Gibson and other Cardinals Hall of Famers in the back of red and white Ford Mustang convertibles.

"The Clydesdales trotting around the warning track might be the most beautiful thing I've ever seen at a ballpark," La Russa told reporters after the game. "I watched them and it was absolutely gorgeous. Stan and Red weren't quite as gorgeous."

After four decades of watching their beloved Cards play in a much loved but worn-out park, loyal St. Louis fans were the latest to celebrate a new wave of ballpark construction in the heartland. PNC Park in Pittsburgh and Miller Park in Milwaukee opened for business in 2001, and Great American Ball Park in Cincinnati came on the scene in 2003.

Just as the Cardinals chose to honor Stan "The Man" Musial with a statue outside Gate 3, other clubs also paid homage to the past while embracing the future. Fans going into PNC Park in Pittsburgh passed statues of icons Roberto Clemente, Honus Wagner and Willie Stargell, along with a "Hitter's Hands" sculpture in honor of Ralph Kiner. The right-field fence stands 21 feet high, recognizing Clemente's No. 21.

Many observers called Pittsburgh's new park the most eye-catching in the game. It had a stunning view of the city skyline beyond the Roberto Clemente Bridge, and the exterior was

Fans pour into the new Busch Stadium for the Cardinals' home opener on April 10, 2006. Once inside, they saw St. Louis defeat Milwaukee in the first game at the new park.

made of limestone rather than the more conventional brick. The park was a stark departure from the antiseptic concrete bowl at Three Rivers Stadium, home to the Pirates and the NFL's Steelers for three decades. "Everybody's jaw drops when they see this place," said then-Pirates infielder John Wehner. "It's just perfect. You couldn't ask for anything more."

PITCHER'S PARADISE

SAN DIEGO PADRES General Manager Kevin Towers, a self-professed dirt and grass devotee, is predisposed toward ballparks with a neighborhood feel and a sense of history. In Towers' world, nothing beats stepping onto the diamond at Wrigley Field for BP just before the anthem plays and the beer lines form.

That said, a Saturday evening with an ocean breeze, snacking on fish tacos, and Adrian Gonzalez digging a toe into the batter's box might come close.

The Padres unveiled a West Coast patch of heaven in 2004 with Petco Park and its views of the San Diego Bay, Balboa Park and the city skyline. Towers summed it up nicely prior to the '04 home opener when he said, "I sat in right field and I had chills."

Petco borrows from several venues. The Western Metal Supply building in left field is reminiscent of the B&O warehouse in Baltimore, and the bleacher seats on the roof provide a touch of Wrigley. Antoine Predock, the New Mexico–based architect who designed Petco, even used sand-colored stone and stucco to simulate the look of the nearby La Jolla cliffs.

With its spacious dimensions — including 334 feet down the left-field line and 411 feet to the right-field alley — Petco is perfect for the fan who enjoys defense and pitching.

SPACIOUS CONFINES

When the Tigers unveiled Comerica Park at the dawn of the millennium, people praised its many fan-friendly features. But like Petco Park, many players lamented its size — except, that is, for pitchers and Bobby Abreu, the only players for whom the park seemed perfectly tailored.

The Detroit club had moved from a hitter's paradise in Tiger Stadium to a new home of daunting proportions just in time for the 2000 season. Comerica's center-field fence was built 420 feet from home plate, and the left-field fence eventually had to be shortened to 345 feet to better accommodate hitters.

But one hitter who needed no special assistance in Detroit was then-Phillies slugger Abreu. The outfielder took the limelight at Comerica in 2005, doing what few batters were able to do at the Tigers' home field: He hit home runs — a lot of them. At the 2005 Home Run Derby, he took the liberty to launch a record-setting 41 homers — 24 in the first round alone — toward Detroit's downtown skyline. And although he ultimately defeated then-hometown favorite Ivan Rodriguez to win the contest, Abreu's was a show even Tigers fans could appreciate that July.

HITTERS' HAVENS

HITTERS WHO GROUSED about far-flung fences and unfavorable conditions in some parks didn't have much reason to complain about other new locales. Great American Ball Park in Cincinnati, which opened in 2003, and Citizens Bank Park, home of the Phillies since 2004, quickly gained reputations as hitter-friendly venues.

Phillies General Manager Ed Wade promised that the team's new park would be "fair," but the smallish dimensions became a source of intrigue among the local media. Two *Philadelphia Inquirer* reporters even tagged along behind members of the grounds crew as they remeasured the distances to the outfield walls to confirm they were posted accurately.

"It might be a better place to hit than Coors Field," the Giants' J.T. Snow said during the park's first year. "It's really small. Guys were giddy after batting practice."

The Phillies would move the fences back a bit to create a more equitable environment, but the park still played small. The same could be said for Great American Ball Park, which took a toll on pitchers' confidence and ERAs. Cincinnati hitters took aim at the outfield seats, and the Reds annually ranked among the NL leaders in homers at home. In 2007, more longballs were hit in Philadelphia (241) and Cincinnati (231) than any other park.

The focus on offense couldn't obscure the delight that fans and players took in the parks,

Petco Park has been an ideal yard for pitchers and baseball traditionalists alike.

which had a charm and sense of intimacy that were lacking in the old Astroturf mausoleums.

"The scoreboard is so big and so high," marveled Philadelphia catcher Mike Lieberthal after getting his first glimpse of Citizens Bank Park. "The brick wall in center field, the Liberty Bell, the grass … it's amazing."

THROWBACKS

MAJOR LEAGUE BASEBALL began its "retro" ballpark phase during the 1990s, when many stadiums were built with brick exteriors and interior nooks, crannies and other idiosyncratic touches that were nonexistent during the concrete saucer era of the 1970s. The spate of construction continued at the start of the new millennium — in triplicate. There was a great sense of anticipation as new parks arrived in Houston, Detroit and San Francisco in 2000. Each site had a unique personality and novel features to enhance the in-game experience.

San Francisco's AT&T Park, which opened as Pac Bell Park and then became SBC Park, is the first privately financed park since Dodger Stadium in 1962. Whatever you called it, the Giants' home was noteworthy for its location on the water. As boats circled McCovey Cove in search of Splash Hits by lefty sluggers, the party-like atmosphere was hard to miss.

"This ballpark will not be the biggest, not the most expensive, not the most luxurious," Giants Owner Peter Magowan said before the stadium opened. "Just the best: small, cozy, urban, brick and steel, with a grass field and a short right-field porch where sluggers like Barry Bonds can send home runs right into San Francisco Bay."

Houston also aimed to combine the best of both worlds: A retractable roof shielded people from the sun and searing Texas heat while bringing open-air baseball back to Houston for the first time in 36 years. And the grass field was a welcome change from the Astrodome's Astroturf. Minute Maid Park (originally Enron Field) abutted Houston's historic Union Station, and a replica 19th-century train circled the outfield wall in response to homers and wins by the Astros. Tal's Hill, a Crosley Field–like incline in straightaway center field, also generated attention.

A BIG APRIL IN THE BIG APPLE

AFTER YEARS OF waiting, both New York clubs christened new parks in April 2009. While each structure was long on creature comforts, they played differently between the lines.

The new Yankee Stadium featured an abundance of concession stand options for fans, a spacious press box and gargantuan clubhouses. "It's an awfully big locker room," said Yankees Hall of Famer Yogi Berra. "To talk to a guy you have to walk half a mile."

Things were cozier between the lines, though, as hitters and pitchers adjusted to the sight of baseballs sailing over fences. The Yankees and their first two opponents, the Indians and A's, combined for 83 runs and 23 homers in the first six games at the new park.

The Mets' new home in Citi Field, in contrast, was a more pitcher-friendly venue, with spacious outfield gaps and high walls that made home runs a challenge for hitters.

"I juiced the ball just right of center field as hard as the Lord can let me hit a ball, and it hit midway up the wall for a double," said Atlanta's Chipper Jones after the Braves' first visit.

While Citi Field was designed to pay tribute to Brooklyn's Ebbets Field, the new park in the Bronx resembles its predecessor, the original pre–1970s renovation Yankee Stadium.

"CITIZENS BANK PARK MIGHT BE A BETTER PLACE TO HIT THAN COORS FIELD. GUYS WERE GIDDY AFTER BATTING PRACTICE." J.T. SNOW

Opposite: The Phillies and their fans felt right at home in their cozy new ballpark during a 5-2 victory against the Brewers in Game 2 of the 2008 NLDS. Next spread: Fans crowd San Francisco's McCovey Cove, hoping for a home run splash.

Commissioner Bud Selig, who attended the home opener, said the park struck just the right balance between adherence to tradition and a more modern-day feel.

"You really have to be clever about it," Selig said. "Let's be honest — Yankee Stadium was the most famous sports cathedral in the world. Do you want to preserve it? You bet you do, because you're preserving the legacy of the franchise."

GRAND OPENING

AFTER A LENGTHY odyssey from Montreal to contraction limbo to rickety old RFK Stadium, the Washington Nationals got themselves a shiny new home to start the 2008 season. For an organization that had come to regard itself as baseball's vagabond, it was a sweet Opening Day for sure.

Nationals Park, the team's new playground, featured modern amenities big and small. Players dressed at lockers built of cherry wood, separated by overhead columns made of Louisville Sluggers. And with high-speed Internet access and iPod charging stations at their disposal, the future was truly upon them.

"They got their money's worth here," Nationals reliever Ray King said before the grand opening. "As players, we appreciate where we've come from to where we are. This stadium really gives the Washington Nationals a home."

And Opening Day at that home surely was an event. President George W. Bush threw out the ceremonial first pitch, and Commissioner Bud Selig gave Nationals Park high praise.

In the park's first game, the Nationals made sure to christen their new yard in style. With the score tied, 2-2, in the bottom of the ninth inning, third baseman Ryan Zimmerman launched a 1-0 fastball from Braves reliever Peter Moylan over the left-field fence for his fourth career walk-off homer. That gave Washington pitcher Jon Rauch the first-ever win in Nationals park.

Team President Stan Kasten, who spent the evening monitoring the concession lines and making sure everything was in proper working order, laughed when asked if the Nationals might consider renaming the new park "The House That Zim Built" — an obvious reference to old Yankee Stadium's nickname, "The House That Ruth Built."

"I'm not ready to do that yet, but everything is a sponsorship deal," Kasten joked. "It could be arranged for a price."

Opposite: The new Yankee Stadium kept a classic feel, while providing new amenities. This page: Washington's new park helped the Nationals forge an identity. Next spread: The entrance to the Mets' Citi Field resembles Ebbets Field.

CHAPTER 4
PITCHING DOMINANCE

The decade began with Pedro Martinez throwing four "plus" pitches at Fenway Park and Curt Schilling and Randy Johnson striking up a mutually beneficial partnership in the Arizona desert. Roger Clemens remained productive into his forties, Mike Mussina pocketed his first 20-win season at age 39 before retiring, and Johan Santana's strikeout-to-walk ratio had to be seen and double-checked to be believed. These aces hardly seemed troubled by ballpark fences getting closer, bat heads getting whippier, and a strike zone growing too small for some pitchers' tastes. Such inherent disadvantages couldn't prevent these guys from doing some memorable things on the mound.

ZEROS

BRANDON WEBB ISN'T a very complicated person. He enjoys playing the guitar in his spare time, rooting for the University of Kentucky basketball team during the winter, and throwing sinkers as if they're coming off an assembly line. Webb has been known to throw the pitch about 90 percent of the time in some games. When it's working properly, life can be awfully dull in the Arizona Diamondbacks' outfield.

"There are times when you want to pull up a lawn chair, order up a drink from the bar and check out all the chicks at the pool," Arizona outfielder Eric Byrnes once commented, referencing the pool beyond the outfield wall at Chase Field.

If any of Webb's teammates stopped paying attention in the summer of 2007, they missed a compelling run at history. Webb cut a swath through National League lineups in July and August, throwing 42 consecutive shutout innings. He became the first pitcher to throw three straight complete-game shutouts since Roger Clemens achieved the feat in 1998 for the Toronto Blue Jays.

The streak, which Milwaukee's Prince Fielder ended with a first-inning RBI single on Aug. 22, was the fifth longest in the Majors since 1940. Orel Hershiser, Don Drysdale, Bob Gibson and Sal Maglie are the only hurlers to put up a longer run of zeros than Webb strung together.

Arizona Manager Bob Melvin, who had refrained from speaking to Webb during the streak for fear of jinxing it, greeted his staff ace at the dugout steps at the end of the first inning and said, "Way to go. Now move past it, will you?'"

It took some of Webb's teammates a little longer to fully digest the spectacle that they had witnessed.

Webb put together one of the most dominant strings of games ever when he threw 42 consecutive scoreless innings during the 2007 season.

"To do what that guy did in that stretch — three complete game shutouts in a row?" said Diamondbacks catcher Chris Snyder. "I don't even know how to describe it."

SAN DIEGO SUPERSTAR

JAKE PEAVY PRESENTS quite an array of obstacles for hitters, with his mid-90s fastball, a slider and cutter that approach the plate with Wiffle Ball–like movement, and a cross-body delivery that makes each pitch difficult to see coming out of his hand. When everything is working in harmony, Peavy is capable of generating quite a breeze from batters.

San Diego's staff ace was never better than on the night of April 25, 2007, when he struck out 16 Arizona hitters over seven innings in a 3-2 loss to the Diamondbacks. Peavy struck out the side in the second, third *and* fourth innings — nine straight batters — to fall one short of Tom Seaver and Eric Gagne's record of 10 consecutive strikeouts. The feat was particularly impressive given that eight straight Arizona hitters went down swinging before Chad Tracy took a called third strike. The K streak finally ended when Eric Byrnes drew a leadoff walk on a 3-2 count in the fifth.

Peavy also conducted himself like an All-Star teammate on his big night against Arizona, expressing wholehearted support for Trevor Hoffman after the Padres' closer allowed a two-run homer to Stephen Drew to blow the save in San Diego's 3-2 loss.

"I love Hoffy to death, and he knows I'm in his corner," Peavy said.

Peavy went on to win the NL's pitching Triple Crown in 2007 with 19 victories, a 2.54 ERA and 240 strikeouts, taking home the Cy Young Award in a unanimous vote.

DYNAMIC FOURSOME

AS THE CHICAGO White Sox starters set a new standard for longevity during the 2005 postseason, the relievers dealt with an unexpected side effect: terminal boredom.

Chicago starters Jose Contreras, Mark Buehrle, Jon Garland and Freddy Garcia worked 44.1 of a possible 45 frames as the White Sox eliminated the Angels in five games in the American League Championship Series. The group also became the first foursome to throw consecutive complete-game victories in the same postseason since Jack Pfiester, Ed Reulbach, Orval Overall and Mordecai "Three Finger" Brown did it for the Chicago Cubs in the 1907 World Series. Neal Cotts was the only reliever to appear for the White Sox in the Series, with a seven-pitch cameo in Game 1.

WHITE SOX STARTING PITCHERS' 2005 ALCS STATS						
Pitcher	Game	IP	H	R	BB	K
Jose Contreras	1	8.1	7	3	0	4
Mark Buehrle	2	9	5	1	0	4
Jon Garland	3	9	4	2	1	7
Freddy Garcia	4	9	6	2	1	5
Jose Contreras	5	9	5	3	2	2

"Guys talk about what they did last night, what's going on with the family and stuff like that," Cotts said of the relievers. "Once you get bored with that, you try to tell jokes and start making fun of each other to kill time."

In their four straight complete games to close out the Series, Chicago's starters threw a total of 99, 118, 116 and 114 pitches, respectively.

"We watch pitch counts and innings, but our day isn't ruled by the pitch count," said Don Cooper, the White Sox's pitching coach. "It's a pretty novel way to make a decision, don't you think?"

Although Chicago's starters weren't quite as dominant in the World Series, they still posted a 2-0 record with a 2.86 ERA, and the well-armed White Sox swept Houston for the franchise's first title in 88 years.

San Diego's Peavy won a Cy Young Award and the pitching Triple Crown in 2007.

ABSOLUTELY PERFECT

THE BRAVES HAD to feel a bit disoriented after striking out 18 times in a 3-1 loss to Milwaukee's Ben Sheets on May 16, 2004. After an off day, Atlanta had no idea that it could get worse. Arizona's Randy Johnson — world champion, strikeout king, Cy Young Award winner and author of a no-hitter in 1990 — became the oldest pitcher ever to throw a perfect game.

Johnson, 40, dominated the Braves, striking out 13, going to just one three-ball count, and setting down Atlanta's Eddie Perez on a 98-mph fastball to end the contest. The lefty's 14-year gap between no-nos was the longest ever. He joined Cy Young, Jim Bunning, Hideo Nomo and Nolan Ryan as one of five pitchers to throw no-hitters in both the AL and NL.

"This is one of those nights where a superior athlete was on top of his game," Arizona Manager Bob Brenly said. "There was a tremendous rhythm out there. His focus, his concentration, his stuff, everything was as good as it could possibly be."

Johnson's was the only perfecto of the decade until July 23, 2009, when he was joined by the White Sox's Mark Buehrle. Playing against the defending AL champion Rays, Buehrle struck out six, but needed a great defensive play to stay perfect. With no outs in the ninth, Tampa's Gabe Kapler hit a shot to left-center field. But center fielder DeWayne Wise, in as a defensive replacement, tracked it down and snagged it just as it was going over the wall. A wise defensive move indeed. Buehrle went on to set a Big League record for most consecutive batters retired (45) by sitting down the first 17 Twins in his next start.

BACK IN THE GAME

CLIFF LEE WAS understandably elated after learning that he had just joined former Cleveland teammate CC Sabathia to win the Indians' second straight Cy Young Award in 2008.

"This is the pinnacle," Lee told reporters on a conference call. "This is where every pitcher wants to be. He wants to be taking a phone call like this about winning the Cy Young. I'd like to do it again. I'd like to make a habit of it."

The experience beat spending much of the previous summer playing for the Indians' Triple-A affiliate in Buffalo, N.Y. Lee was one down-and-out lefty in 2007. He posted a 5-8 record with a 6.29 ERA in 16 starts, and pitched badly enough that the Indians optioned him to Buffalo for a refresher course in July. When the Indians reached the postseason, Lee's name wasn't on the playoff roster. But he channeled his energies into a comeback, and his hard work was evident in the results.

Previous spread: Buehrle pitches in the ninth against the Rays, moments from completing his 2009 perfecto. This page: Johnson is mobbed by teammates after his perfect game in 2004. Opposite: Halladay led the Blue Jays' rotation for most of the decade, preparing meticulously for his starts.

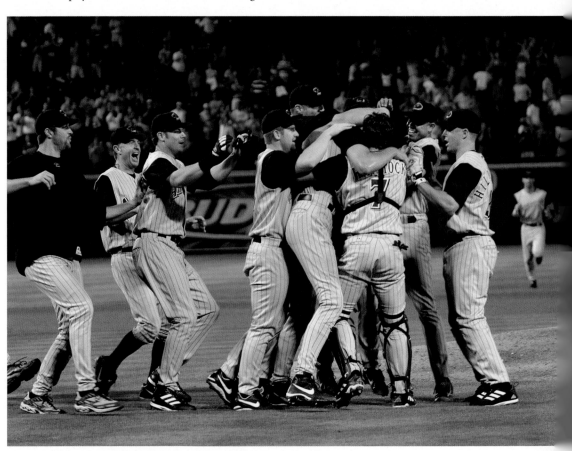

Given a fresh start in 2008, Lee's .880 winning percentage tied Brooklyn's Preacher Roe for fifth best in a season by a tcher with at least 20 decisions. Only Greg Maddux, Randy Johnson, Ron Guidry and Lefty Grove posted higher per- ntages in a season. Lee started for the AL in the All-Star Game at Yankee Stadium, reeled off 11 straight victories from d-July to mid-September, and became the first Cleveland pitcher to win 20 games since Gaylord Perry did it in 1974.

HE ROYS

s TORONTO STARTER Roy Halladay moved closer to his free agency "walk year" in the spring of 2009, General Manager ?. Ricciardi was so in awe of his staff ace's talent and work ethic that he couldn't consider toning down the praise for ture contract leverage.

"He's the best," Ricciardi said. "No one prepares like him, and no one competes like him. He's the epitome of what No. 1 should be."

Halladay, known to friends and admirers as "Doc," is widely hailed for his competitiveness and consistency. But while lks in Toronto regard him as baseball's premier starter, some people in Houston might contend that he's not baseball's ost accomplished "Roy."

From 2001–08, Astros starter Roy Oswalt led all Big League pitchers with 129 victories and ranked third with a 3.13 RA. Those 129 wins over the first eight years of his career surpassed the totals for Hall of Famers Don Drysdale, Warren ahn, Whitey Ford, Don Sutton and Bob Gibson over the same span.

"He's a special kid," teammate Roger Clemens said of Oswalt in 2007. "He's got electric stuff. And I think every year he arns more. He makes more adjustments. And that's what's going to allow him, if he wants, to pitch 15 to 20 years."

Physically, the two Roys aren't similar. At 6'6" and 225 pounds, Halladay has a classic pitcher's body. Oswalt, in con- ast, is an undersized righty at 6 feet, 185 pounds. Halladay was a 1995 first-round pick by Toronto, while Oswalt went the 23rd round in 1996 as a "draft and follow" by Houston out of Holmes Community College in Mississippi.

Differences aside, the Roys are linked by their intensity and focus. Halladay's Toronto teammates have learned to give him ace as he prepares for starts, and Oswalt's fellow Astros see a killer instinct in him that belies his small-town demeanor.

"Roy has a laid-back personality until he gets on the mound," said Jackie Moore, who managed Oswalt in the Minor Leagues. "He's quite a competitor. I heard him make the statement once that he doesn't even like anybody passing him on the highway."

PEERLESS

IN THE SUMMER of 1999, Pedro Martinez posted a 23-4 record with a 2.07 ERA for the Boston Red Sox and joined Randy Johnson and Gaylord Perry as one of three pitchers to win the Cy Young Award in each league. Then Martinez did something even more amazing: He raised his game a notch.

Although Martinez's 18-6 record in 2000 wasn't quite as stunning as his '99 mark, he recorded a 1.74 ERA — the lowest by an American League starter since Luis Tiant's 1.60 in 1968. The Yankees' Roger Clemens finished a distant second to Martinez in the ERA race at 3.70.

"I think he had a better year this year," said Red Sox Manager Jimy Williams. "You can't just look at his wins and losses."

Martinez entered into heady company with his sustained record of excellence. He joined Clemens, Steve Carlton, Greg Maddux, Tom Seaver, Sandy Koufax and Jim Palmer on the list of pitchers with at least three Cy Young Awards. Randy Johnson would eventually join that esteemed fraternity, as well.

"It was the confidence to have it all going your way, where you felt like you were on top of everything," Martinez said while pitching for the Mets later in his career. "Now that I'm facing the other side of the coin, I can really tell what the difference is."

OFF THE CHARTS

Just once in 2000, against Kansas City, did Pedro Martinez allow more than three runs in a game. "How did you do it?" reporters asked the Royals' Mike Sweeney after that game. "I have no idea," he answered. Here are some of Martinez's most memorable performances from that season:

- May 12 vs. Orioles: 9 IP, 2 H, 0 R, 0 BB, 15 K
- May 28 vs. Yankees: 9 IP, 4 H, 0 R, 1 BB, 9 K
- July 23 vs. White Sox: 9 IP, 6 H, 0 R, 0 BB, 15 K
- Aug. 29 vs. Devil Rays: 9 IP, 1 H, 0 R, 0 BB, 13 K

ACE OF QUEENS

IF ANYONE HAD ever questioned Johan Santana's toughness, he proved his mettle with a bravura performance for the Mets late in 2008. With a playoff berth on the line and the Mets desperate for a win, Santana — on a knee that would require surgery a week later — took the ball on short rest and pitched a complete-game three-hitter to beat the Marlins, 2-0, at Shea Stadium on the penultimate day of the season.

Mets Manager Jerry Manuel, who had long since run out of ways to describe Santana, began his post-game press conference by uttering the word "wow" four times in succession.

"I think if I had to describe that one, I'd say that was 'gangsta,'" Manuel said. "That's serious 'gangsta' right there."

If "gangsta" equates to two Cy Young Awards, three strikeout titles, three ERA crowns, three All-Star appearances and a Gold Glove in a five-year span, then Manuel is free from conjuring up any new superlatives anytime soon.

Santana, a resourceful lefty from Venezuela, put a lot of bats in cold storage after Minnesota acquired him from Florida by trade following baseball's Rule 5 draft in 1999. He overwhelmed hitters with a lethal mix of fastballs, sliders, "Bugs Bunny" change-ups and impeccable control, and became a 20-game winner at age 25.

The Mets traded four prospects to Minnesota for their ace in February 2008, then signed Santana to a six-year contract. At the time, the deal was the most lucrative ever for a pitcher. All it took was one season for the Mets to realize they had made a wise investment.

Martinez posted a mind-boggling 1.74 ERA for the Red Sox in 2000 to win his third Cy Young Award.

CHAPTER 5
SLUGGERS

Ryan Howard has a twin brother and played the trombone in his high school band. These pieces of trivia make for great conversation — until he unloads a 450-foot shot into the upper deck at Citizens Bank Park. The home run might have lost some cachet as the decade progressed, but sluggers have a way of capturing our imagination with their majestic swings and game-changing heroics. With the possible exception of a Carl Crawford triple to the gap, is there anything in baseball more beautiful to watch than a Ken Griffey Jr. follow-through?

COMEBACK KID

WHEN JOSH HAMILTON arrived at the Rangers' Spring Training camp in 2008, he began hitting one drive after another in batting practice while his new teammates strained for superlatives to describe his power.

"I've never seen anyone as gifted as him," said Texas second baseman Ian Kinsler. "He was born to play this game."

They had no idea. Hamilton's act played well at Rangers camp in Surprise, Ariz., but it was nothing compared to the show he put on in the House that Ruth Built before the 2008 All-Star Game. Hamilton staged a power display at the State Farm Home Run Derby that was so profound, the crowd at Yankee Stadium, and media for that matter, barely noticed or cared that he finished second.

Hamilton peppered the outfield seats with a single-round record 28 home runs in the first stanza, all but assuring him a spot in the finals. But by then, he was exhausted and fell, 5-3, to Minnesota's Justin Morneau in the finale.

After collecting the trophy, Morneau conceded that his performance was merely an afterthought to the main event. Overall, he was out-homered, 35-22, but won because the format calls for all totals to be wiped clean before the final head-to-head matchup.

"I think everyone will remember Josh Hamilton more than they'll remember I won," Morneau said. "I'm just glad I was a part of the whole thing."

Hamilton had been the central figure in a season-long fairy tale in Arlington leading up to the All-Star Game. He arrived in New York with a Major League–leading 95 RBI and the support of countless well-wishers who were rooting for him in his return to baseball following a multi-year battle with drugs and alcohol.

Hamilton hit a record 28 home runs in the first round of the Home Run Derby at Yankee Stadium in 2008.

Hamilton was joined at the Derby by Claybon Counsil, a 71-year-old American Legion coach who used to throw him batting practice at home in North Carolina. Their comfort level was clear, as Hamilton drove Counsil's pitches to the nether reaches of Yankee Stadium. At one point, he homered on 13 straight swings, reaching 504 and 518 feet.

The anticlimactic ending didn't spoil the moment for Hamilton, who told reporters about a dream he'd had in 2005 about taking part in a Home Run Derby at Yankee Stadium. Reality, it turns out, was an upgrade over the dream.

"In the backyard, it used to be Yankee Stadium," Hamilton said. "I used to be Babe Ruth, Mickey Mantle, Joe DiMaggio. This is awesome."

POWER HOUSE

THE BIG KID from St. Louis faced high expectations when he arrived in Philadelphia in 2006. He was replacing popular slugger Jim Thome in a city never known for its patience.

But Ryan Howard found a way to score points with the locals, 400 feet at a time.

Howard, physically imposing at 6-foot-4, 260 pounds, kept winning awards while establishing himself as one of baseball's premier power hitters. He knocked 22 home runs in 88 games to win the National League Rookie of the Year Award in 2005, then launched 58 homers to beat out St. Louis's Albert Pujols for NL MVP honors the next year.

Howard easily surpassed Hall of Famer Mike Schmidt's Phillies franchise record of 48 home runs in a season. He also joined Cal Ripken Jr. as one of two players to follow up a Rookie of the Year Award with a Most Valuable Player Award (Dustin Pedroia has since joined them).

Opposing pitchers quickly recognized the danger in pitching to Howard. He was quick enough to pull inside pitches over the right-field wall, and strong and gifted enough to power the ball over the fence in left-center field. No ballpark in baseball could hold him.

"He's our carrier," said Phillies Manager Charlie Manuel. "He's the guy who puts up the big numbers. He's the guy that knocks in the 130 to 160 RBI. He's the guy who's big in the moment. He bears down. He wants to be up there. He strives to drive runs in."

FAST ROAD TO 500

HOME RUN TROTS had always come naturally to Alex Rodriguez. He hit 36 homers as a 20-year-old in his first full season with the Mariners in 1996, and topped 40 homers six times and 50 twice during his next seven seasons, split between Seattle and Texas.

FOUNDING FATHERS

When Babe Ruth hit a home run off Cleveland's Willis Hudlin on Aug. 11, 1929, in Cleveland, he forged a place for himself in history. This blast was different from any other — it was his 500th, and it established Ruth as the founding member of the prestigious 500-home run club. In 5,801 at-bats, Ruth achieved a milestone that no player before him came close to reaching. The Bambino was 34 when he found himself on Cleveland's Lexington Avenue trading an autographed ball with a young fan in exchange for the very piece of history he created.

Although he played several years after Ruth, Mickey Mantle shared a monumental accomplishment with the fellow Yankees great in 1967. Besides Ruth, just four players before Mantle had achieved the 500-homer feat. The Mick managed to leave his 500th mark at home in the Cathedral, launching a game-winning home run off Orioles pitcher Stu Miller. His May 14th blast inducted Mantle as the first switch-hitter to join the club.

Rodriguez (center) celebrates at home plate with Abreu (53) and Jeter after hitting career home run No. 500 on Aug. 4, 2007.

Arriving in the Bronx in 2004, Rodriguez continued along the express lane to his 500th homer. At just 32 years old — 328 days younger than Jimmie Foxx — he became the youngest player in history to reach the mark. Still, the week before the milestone felt like an eternity. As the media glare increased, Rodriguez felt like he was swinging in slow motion. Squeezing the bat progressively tighter, he went nine days and 36 plate appearances before finally pulling the cork on the celebration.

History occurred in the first frame of a 16-8 win over the Royals, when Rodriguez drove a Kyle Davies fastball out of Yankee Stadium. He joined Babe Ruth and Mickey Mantle as the only players ever to hit their 500th home runs in a Yankees uniform.

Rodriguez raised his hands in triumph as he circled the bases, then hugged teammates Derek Jeter and Bobby Abreu, who had scored ahead of him, as he crossed home plate.

"To do it at home and to wear this beautiful uniform that I appreciate and respect so much, it's special," Rodriguez said. "New York is a special place."

MILWAUKEE'S PRINCE

PRINCE FIELDER SEEMED like royalty in Milwaukee in 2007 after becoming the youngest player to hit 50 homers in a season. At 23 years and 139 days old, Fielder overtook Willie Mays' mark by just under a year. No. 50 came on Sept. 25 against the rival Cardinals.

But Fielder's biggest thrill came a month later, when he received a hitting award named for an equally luminous Hall of Famer. Fielder, winner of the Hank Aaron Award in fan balloting as the top offensive player in the NL, basked in words of praise from the award's inspiration and namesake at a ceremony at the World Series in Denver.

"In the 23 years that I played baseball, a lot of players hit an awful lot of home runs but couldn't produce in the clutch, could not hit in the clutch," said Aaron. "Prince did that all year. He carried his ballclub all year."

Fielder ranked second in the NL to teammate Ryan Braun with a .618 slugging percentage, and broke the franchise record of 45 homers in a season shared by Gorman Thomas and Richie Sexson. He also surpassed Milwaukee's record of 47 home runs in a single season, held by former Brave Eddie Mathews.

Fielder hit his 49th and 50th homers in the same game against St. Louis to reach the milestone 363 days ahead of Mays. "It's just an awesome feat," said Fielder, father of two. "Now my kids can know, at one time, their dad was pretty good."

LIKE FATHER, LIKE SON

Despite the many instances of multiple generations of a family playing in the Majors, Cecil and Prince Fielder share a bond that no other father-son duo can boast. Both are members of the 50-home run club, and they are the only such pair in MLB history to achieve the feat.

Prince, a first baseman like his father (who was also a DH), hit his milestone homer in September 2007. In doing so, he set the Brewers' franchise record for home runs in a season, but failed to surpass his father's 51-homer year. But during 2009 All-Star Week in St. Louis, Prince did accomplish one thing his father never did: He won the ever-popular Home Run Derby.

HOME RUN KING

BARRY BONDS WAS the center of attention during three of the most enduring moments of the decade. The first came on Oct. 5, 2001, when he went deep against Chan Ho Park of the Los Angeles Dodgers to break Mark McGwire's single-season home run record of 70. Bonds hit two more longballs in the last days of the season against Los Angeles to establish a new mark of 73.

The second came on May 28, 2006, when Bonds connected against Colorado Rockies pitcher Byung-Hyun Kim for No. 715 to pass Babe Ruth for second place on the all-time home run list.

In 2007, Fielder became the youngest player to hit 50 home runs in a season.

Bonds achieved his ultimate goal on Aug. 7, 2007, when he drove a 3-2 fastball from Washington's Mike Bacsik o the fence in right-center field at AT&T Park to break Hank Aaron's career record of 755 home runs.

As Bonds crossed home plate on the record-setter, he hugged his son, Nikolai, then pointed to the sky in honor of late father, Bobby — a former All-Star himself. Moments later, Aaron appeared on the outfield video screen and congral lated the new home run king on his special night.

"I move over and offer my best wishes to Barry and his family on this historical achievement," Aaron said. "My ho today, as it was on that April evening in 1974, is that the achievement of this record will inspire others to chase th own dreams."

Bonds would go on to hit six more home runs over the final two months of the 2007 season to finish his landma career with 762 longballs. Over 22 Big League seasons and more than 12,000 plate appearances, he established hims as one of the best all-around players ever.

GRAND FINALE

IT SEEMS AS though it would be tough for a single swing to stand out in a 13-0 rout, but Cleveland slugger Tra Hafner made it happen in August 2006, when he tied a Major League record and rekindled some pleasant childho memories with a big fly against the Kansas City Royals.

As a boy in the tiny town of Sykeston, S.D., the Indians' designated hitter can remember watching Don Mattingly a the rest of the Yankees on television. So it meant just a little something extra when he hit his sixth grand slam of 2006 to Mattingly's single-season record. The home run put an exclamation point on a Cleveland onslaught against Kansas City's Lu Hudson. It wasn't until after the first 10 Indians reached base and Cleveland took a 7-0 lead, that outfielder Jason Micha struck out for the first out of the first inning. Hafner followed it up with a shot over the right field fence for grand slam No.

"It's pretty cool to tie a Major League record," Hafner, typically understated, told reporters in the clubhou "Mattingly was one of the best hitters in the game."

Although Hafner still had 45 games to surpass Mattingly, he was unable to put a seventh grand slam in the books.

THE 500 CLUB

WHILE MEMBERSHIP IN baseball's 500–home run club still confers a certain status based on consistent production over time, the fraternity isn't quite as exclusive as it used to be.

At the start of the 2001 season, just 16 players had hit 500 homers. Eight years later, Barry Bonds, Sammy Sosa, Rafael Palmeiro, Ken Griffey Jr., Frank Thomas, Alex Rodriguez, Jim Thome, Manny Ramirez and Gary Sheffield had expanded the list to 25. Griffey and Sosa eventually surpassed 600 home runs, while Bonds finished his career with 762 roundtrippers.

Thome's shot was among the most dramatic. With about 25 friends and relatives in the stands at U.S. Cellular Field in Chicago on Sept. 16, 2007, he hit a two-run shot off Dustin Moseley in the bottom of the ninth inning to give the White Sox a 9-7 victory over the Los Angeles Angels.

Thome was mobbed at home plate, then lifted into the air by teammates Jermaine Dye and Bobby Jenks, who held him on their shoulders during the celebration.

"I would never have imagined doing that as a walk-off," Thome said. "It's amazing to see your teammates standing there. It's like a movie script."

Sheffield knows the feeling. During Spring Training in 2009, he was released by the Detroit Tigers despite sitting on 499 career home runs. Sheffield signed with the Mets before the season opener, and slugged his 500th longball off Milwaukee's Mitch Stetter on April 17 at Citi Field in Queens.

At 40 years and 150 days old, Sheffield became the fourth-oldest player to hit 500 home runs, behind Willie McCovey, Eddie Murray and Ted Williams.

Said the ecstatic Sheffield, "Now I can say I'm in the club and, you know, it's like getting your degree. Nobody can ever take that away from you."

HAFNER CAN REMEMBER WATCHING DON MATTINGLY ON TV. SO IT MEANT SOMETHING EXTRA WHEN HE HIT HIS SIXTH GRAND SLAM OF 2006 TO TIE MATTINGLY'S SINGLE-SEASON RECORD.

Opposite: Bonds hits career home run No. 756 to pass Aaron's all-time record on Aug. 7, 2007.
This page: Hafner tied Mattingly's single-season grand slams record with six in 2006.
Next spread: Thome celebrates his 500th career homer, a walk-off against the Angels on Sept. 16, 2007.

FREE SWINGER

Vladimir Guerrero developed a novel approach to hitting during his youth in the Dominican Republic. And as his Major League career progressed, no amount of fame, riches or All-Star Game appearances was about to change it.

"Ever since I was a little boy, I have been swinging at everything I see that comes near home plate," Guerrero said. "It doesn't really matter whether they're going to give me pitches to hit or not."

Guerrero's comfort zone extends from his shoulders to the tops of his shoes, from the inside corner of the plate to the outside corner — and often beyond. On days when he's feeling particularly adventurous, it might even stretch out of Anaheim's 714 area code. But there's no disputing the effectiveness of his approach.

Guerrero compiled a stunning list of achievements in his first 12 Big League seasons. But the strongest testament to his skill might have come in 2008, when he joined Hall of Famer Lou Gehrig as the second player in history to hit .300 with 25 home runs in 11 straight seasons.

Despite injuries that eventually put a crimp in his speed and defense, Guerrero's free-swinging exuberance is what allowed him to leave his hometown of Nizao Bani and take on the Major Leagues. And with the possible exception of Yogi Berra, bad-ball hitters just don't come any better.

"He's an old-style free swinger," said former Angels outfielder Tim Salmon. "He kind of reminds me of a Roberto Clemente. He seems like he's got it down pretty simple — just rear back and swing as hard as you can. Those guys are fun to watch."

THE MACHINE

In an age of breeze-generating free swingers, St. Louis Cardinals first baseman Albert Pujols is the rarest of birds — an extra-base hit machine who produces staggering power without high strikeout totals. Pujols put up some mind-boggling stats during the decade, and one campaign of particular note came in 2006, when he hit 49 home runs, drove in 137 runs and finished with a slugging percentage of .671. Amazingly, Pujols struck out just 50 times that year, falling just one home run short of joining Johnny Mize of the 1947 New York Giants as the only players to hit 50 homers with fewer than 50 whiffs in a season.

That's no accident. Pujols is happy to let it fly when he's ahead in the count, but he'll also spread out and try to hit the ball up the middle if a single will suffice.

"I get mad when I strike out," Pujols said. "At least if you put the ball in play, a guy can make an error and you give your teammates a chance to drive you in and score a run. When you strike out, you don't even give yourself a chance."

Pujols' knack for making contact with authority is reminiscent of Hall of Famers Stan Musial, Hank Aaron, Mel Ott, Carl Yastrzemski and Babe Ruth, all of whom played two decades or more without a 100-strikeout season.

Guerrero's unique approach to hitting made him one of the most feared batters in the Majors.

GUERRERO'S EXUBERANCE IS WHAT ALLOWED HIM TO TAKE ON THE MAJORS. AND WITH THE POSSIBLE EXCEPTION OF YOGI BERRA, BAD-BALL HITTERS JUST DON'T COME ANY BETTER.

His personal role model is none other than Joe DiMaggio, who hit 361 homers and struck out just 369 times in his career.

"Unbelievable," Pujols said. "Those are sick numbers."

600 FOR 'THE KID'

As Ken Griffey Jr. eased into his mid- and then late 30s, the familiar youthful bounce in his step was hindered by a series of foot, knee and hamstring injuries. Griffey grew accustomed to hearing fans and media members wonder what might have been if only he had been able to remain healthy. But the great ones have a way of surprising people, and Griffey's turn came during an inspired run with Cincinnati from 2005 through 2007, when he enjoyed a second wind and provided flashbacks to his heyday with the Mariners, when he was known as "The Kid."

The big payoff came on June 9, 2008, in Miami, when Griffey drove a 3-1 curveball from Marlins left-handed hurler Mark Hendrickson over the right-field fence to join Barry Bonds, Hank Aaron, Babe Ruth, Willie Mays and Sammy Sosa in baseball's 600–home run club.

"I didn't really think about it running around the bases," Griffey said. "I don't think I even touched any of the bases. I sort of floated around."

After waving to his wife, Melissa, who sat in the stands, Griffey shared a hug in the dugout with his 14-year-old son, Trey, who had been traveling with the Reds during the milestone pursuit. The chase had ended up dragging on slightly longer than Griffey would have preferred. After hitting home run No. 599 against Atlanta, Griffey went homerless for nine days, including three missed starts due to a sore knee, before taking Hendrickson deep in Florida for the mark.

Griffey owed a debt of gratitude to Mays and Aaron for reaching out to him with phone calls and putting his mind at ease about 10 days before the milestone blast.

"They just said, 'Keep going, have some fun. Just be you,'" Griffey recalled after reaching the mark. "I think that helped me a little bit, having those guys make a call to me and trying to settle some of the nerves down."

This page: Griffey is honored for his 600th home run in 2008 with an outfield sign. Opposite: In 2006, Pujols fell just short of joining ranks with Mize, the only ballplayer to hit 50 home runs in a season with fewer than 50 strikeouts.

CHAPTER 6

CHARACTERS OF THE GAME

Conventional wisdom holds that increasingly lucrative contracts and an ever-intrusive media have helped produce a more buttoned-down, corporate-type baseball player. And it's true that you don't see as many idiosyncratic and accessible baseball personalities — such as Mark "The Bird" Fidrych, Joltin' Joe Charboneau or Turk Wendell — making the rounds much anymore. But a scan of Major League rosters in the 2000s would have revealed a stray Sean "The Mayor" Casey chatting incessantly at the first base bag, or Eric Byrnes, with his bird's nest haircut and frenetic personality. These players made the game a little more entertaining — and a heck of a lot more fun.

REVENGE OF THE 'IDIOTS'

THERE'S SOMETHING TO be said for a team that forges an identity over the course of a baseball season. In 2003, the Boston Red Sox bonded by shaving their heads as a group and embracing first baseman Kevin Millar's "Cowboy Up" slogan. A year later they assumed an insurgent mentality against the Yankees through shared slovenliness.

Before Millar and Johnny Damon christened the freewheeling 2004 Sox the "Idiots," Boston players engaged in freedom of expression through their hair. Or lack of it.

When Millar was struggling to put up numbers in June, he dyed his hair a fluorescent shade of blond. When that didn't work, he took the shears to it. And then, when he got tired of being bald and clean shaven, Millar grew a beard that made him look like a deckhand aboard a Norwegian salmon trawler. Trot Nixon sported a modified Mohawk. Manny Ramirez's dreadlocks flopped up and down with every jog he took. Damon was dubbed "Unfrozen Caveman Lawyer," after the old *Saturday Night Live* character, because of his bushy beard and flowing locks.

"I just think there are a bunch of earth pigs on this team," said reliever Curtis Leskanic, who signed with Boston in June of 2004 after being released by Kansas City.

The Boston players felt comfortable cutting it loose because management gave them a long leash, but when Damon arrived at Spring Training with his new, hirsute look, General Manager Theo Epstein received letters from fans urging a crackdown. In the end, Epstein let Damon be himself, on the grounds that freedom of expression was fine provided it didn't intrude upon the team concept. If anything, the Red Sox's zaniness served as a handy stress reliever in a demanding environment. "We're not schoolteachers," Epstein said. "This isn't a private school. This game is supposed to be about winning and fun."

Millar (left) and Ramirez embraced the club's renegade image, and led the Red Sox to the promised land for the first time in more than eight decades.

The hard-driving Sox, impervious to the ever-present talk of "curses" in Boston, dispatched the Angels and Yankees in the first two rounds of the playoffs before sweeping the St. Louis Cardinals in the World Series to end the franchise's 86-year championship drought. In all, after falling behind, 3 games to none, in the ALCS, the Sox reeled off eight straight wins for the crown. It's hard to remember a team that had more fun on the road to a title.

"We have a lot of free spirits in this clubhouse," said first baseman Doug Mientkiewicz, who caught the final out of the World Series on a ground ball to closer Keith Foulke. "They do their own thing, that's for sure."

FISH OUT OF WATER

WHEN THINGS WERE going right, it seemed that someone had forgotten to tell Dontrelle Willis that pitchers are fragile commodities, and should exercise caution for fear of injury or other maladies that might befall pro athletes. Marlins Manager Jeff Torborg learned that first-hand in Spring Training of 2003, when the energetic Willis served notice that he was just a baseball player trapped in a fastball-flinging package.

Willis, 21, was standing on first base in a spring game when teammate Juan Pierre laid down a bunt that was bobbled by the infielder and then thrown away. Willis circled the bases before being thrown out at home by 10 feet. He punctuated his trip with a headfirst slide — a major faux pas for a pitcher. Willis got up, dusted himself off and unexpectedly encountered a face full of Torborg — replaced later in the season by Jack McKeon — who delivered a stern and uncompromising message.

CHANGE OF PLANS

The Florida Marlins were a longshot to reach the playoffs in 2003, especially with a rookie pitcher anchoring the rotation. But the postseason is exactly where 2003 NL Rookie of the Year Dontrelle Willis helped lead his squad.

And if the Marlins were doubted before the playoffs, there were even fewer fans who banked on Florida upsetting the Yankees for the title. With creative managing and guys willing to sacrifice for the team, however, the Marlins shocked the world. Willis, for one, changed from starter to postseason set-up man. "He deserves to start," Manager Jack McKeon said during the World Series. "But on the other hand, he gives us that power left-hander out of the bullpen."

Willis thrived with the move. In three Fall Classic relief appearances, Willis kept the Yankees to four hits, striking out three. And after holding New York scoreless in 3.2 innings, the freshman and his squad were the unlikely world champs.

"He told me next time it would be a $1,000 fine," Willis said. "I played in A-ball. I don't have $1,000 to give for a slide."

Willis made the jump to the Marlins from Double-A two months later and quickly generated a Fernando Valenzuela–like mania in the summer of 2003. Florida fans loved his energy, his contorted pitching motion, and his penchant for exchanging back-slaps and high-fives in celebration of … well … just about anything.

Willis won 14 games as a rookie and posted a 22-10 record in 2005. Florida traded him to Detroit two years later, but fans in the Sunshine State will never forget that his "Gee, it's-great-to-be-here" sense of wonder about playing in the Majors helped lift the club to the 2003 world championship.

THE MAYOR

WHEN *SPORTS ILLUSTRATED* asked 464 Big Leaguers in May 2007, "Who is the friendliest player in baseball?" Tigers first baseman Sean Casey lapped the field. He received a whopping 46 percent of the vote compared to 22 percent combined for Jim Thome, Mike Sweeney, Dave Roberts and David Ortiz — the next four players mentioned.

Casey received the nickname "The Mayor" as a college player in the Cape Cod League, and it was a natural fit. He routinely engaged opponents in conversation when they dropped by his post at first, and he was so personable that they couldn't help but reciprocate.

Marlins management tried to get Willis to act the role of the pitcher, but nothing could stop him from diving after balls and into bases.

Casey batted .302 in a 12-year career with Cincinnati, Detroit and three other organizations. But despite those enviable statistics, he'll likely be remembered by many as the game's quintessential nice guy. In September 1998, Casey and Chicago Cubs outfielder Henry Rodriguez were so engrossed in a discussion that Rodriguez was oblivious when Cincinnati pitcher Jason Bere threw over to first base.

"I felt so bad when we picked him off," Casey said. "Henry was chatting at me, getting his lead, and I was chatting at him, and he didn't even move. I put the tag on him and said, 'Sorry about that.' He wasn't mad. What are you going to do?"

HONEST OZZIE

OZZIE GUILLEN'S MAIN objective each year is to lead the Chicago White Sox to a division title, roll through the playoffs and then win the World Series — as the Sox did in 2005. Guillen hopes to finish each season with a champagne celebration and a parade.

Thinking longer term, Guillen has another, more cosmic goal in mind.

"I hope I die on the field," he said. "I hope when I walk to change the pitcher, I drop dead and that's it."

Whenever and wherever Guillen departs, he'll leave behind a trail of devoted admirers, rankled opponents and grateful reporters who took great pleasure in turning on their tape recorders and listening to him go.

From the moment he took over as Chicago's manager in 2004, Guillen rarely kept an opinion to himself. Over the span of several years, he was involved in real or manufactured controversies with players Magglio Ordonez, Frank Thomas and Nick Swisher; opposing managers Buck Showalter and Phil Garner; opposing coaches Dave Duncan, Mariano Duncan and Andy Van Slyke; umpires Phil Cuzzi and Hunter Wendelstedt; and Chicago media personalities Jay Mariotti and Mike North.

And that's only a partial list.

A freewheeling quote machine in a tight-lipped, politically correct world, Guillen values one attribute among all others.

"I never lie to any of my players," he said. "I think that's my problem, being too honest." He might regard it as a problem — to everybody else, it's entertainment.

This page: Guillen, during one of his more serene moments. The Pale Hose skipper has a wild side, but fans can't argue with the results. Next spread: Neither rain, nor sleet, nor outfield wall can stop Arizona's Byrnes.

KID STUFF

WITH FITNESS FREAKS and workout warriors populating clubhouses around the Majors, Padres closer Heath Bell wasn't afraid to be perceived as a guy who enjoyed a little couch time. For years, one of Bell's favorite T-shirts bore the inscription: "I'm in shape. Round is a shape."

Upon arrival at Spring Training in 2009, Bell shared a different sort of tale. He told reporters that he had dropped 30 pounds over the winter, going from 275 to 245, after he stood on his kids' Nintendo Wii Fit game and the device told him he was "obese."

Bell has never met a gadget or a gizmo that was too juvenile for his tastes. He named his fantasy football team "Toys 'R' Us," and has publicly expressed an affinity for Legos, Nerf footballs, Big Wheels and G.I. Joe action figures.

Call Bell immature, and he's likely to take it as a compliment.

"Everybody has always said, 'You're kind of weird,'" Bell said. "Most of my friends can say I'm out there. My family would say I'm out there."

That free-spirited mindset came in handy when Bell replaced franchise icon Trevor Hoffman as San Diego's closer in 2009. He arrived with his very own theme song — "Blow Me Away" by Breaking Benjamin — and a self-described split personality. "When the game starts I want to tear your head off, but I'm one of the nicest guys I know," Bell said.

WALLBANGER

ERIC BYRNES COLLECTS nicknames the way Ichiro Suzuki collects base hits.

He's been called the "Human Crash Test Dummy" for his aggressive, occasionally reckless pursuit of fly balls in the outfield. One writer observed that Byrnes' disheveled hairstyle resembles a "haystack after a tornado." And Byrnes has also lugged around the sobriquet "Pigpen." No clarification is required after one look at the soiled laundry beside his locker.

In the Dominican Republic, where he played winter ball for several years, Byrnes was such a hit in the town of Licey that the locals called him "Captain America."

"I struggled and I almost got booed out of the country," Byrnes said. "Then we won the championship and all was great again. I couldn't go out of the hotel without a mob coming up either wanting to break bottles over my head or hoist me on their shoulders."

Stories? Byrnes has a few. He'll tell you about the time that he and slugger Carlos Pena were on their way to a game and they encountered a flock of chickens in the middle of a downtown Santo Domingo street. They got out of the car, began chasing poultry, and turned it into a game called "Who Can Catch the Chicken?"

Major Leaguers don't come any less pretentious. When the kids from Chandler, Ariz., returned from the Little League World Series in 2007, Byrnes invited the entire group over to his house for a barbecue and pool party.

Byrnes takes an almost perverse pride in his obliviousness to walls and other obstacles, but even he concedes there's a time for discretion. Sacrificing one's body to steal a run and

> "I STRUGGLED AND I ALMOST GOT BOOED OUT OF THE COUNTRY. THEN WE WON THE CHAMPIONSHIP AND ALL WAS GREAT AGAIN. I COULDN'T GO OUT OF THE HOTEL WITHOUT A MOB COMING UP TO ME." ERIC BYRNES

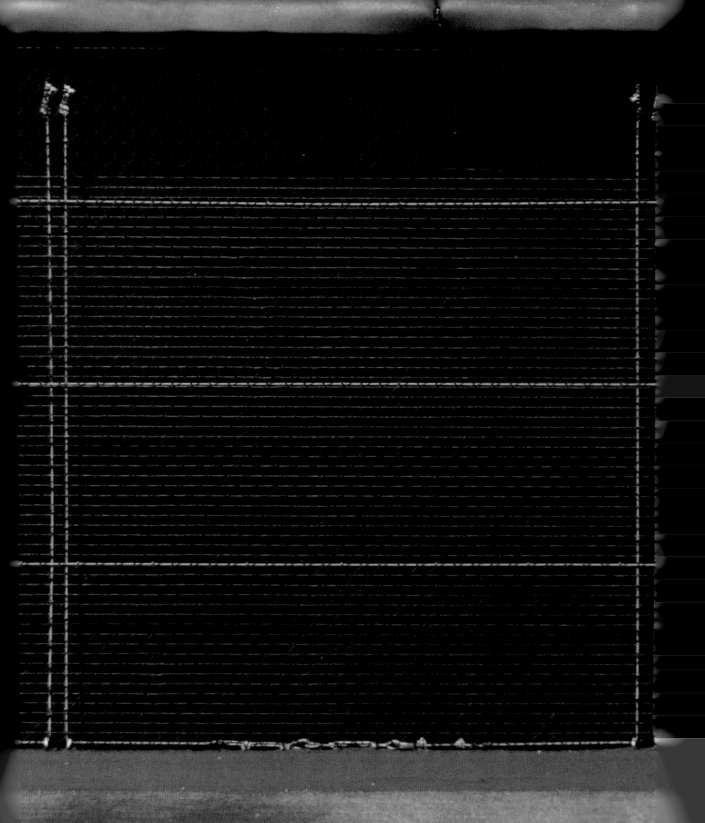

help the pitcher is a given. Face plants just for the fun of it are not. "There's a difference," Byrnes said, "between being aggressive and suicidal."

THE AGITATOR

WHITE SOX MANAGER Ozzie Guillen wanted to say something complimentary about catcher A.J. Pierzynski, even if it didn't quite come out that way. "If you play against A.J., you hate him," Guillen observed in 2006. "If you play with him, you hate him less."

No matter which side you play for, rest assured that Pierzynski will wind up in the middle of the action somewhere. The agitator in Pierzynski might prompt him to jog over the mound on his way back to the bench after an out, just to rankle the opposing pitcher.

It can also happen in memorable, confrontational ways. During a White Sox–Cubs Interleague game in 2006, Pierzynski crashed into fellow catcher Michael Barrett while crossing home plate. Barrett responded by slugging Pierzynski, who raised his hands to acknowledge the cheering crowd at U.S. Cellular Field on his way back to the dugout. "Once Barrett hit him, I think the whole league wanted to give Barrett a pat on the back," White Sox pitcher Mark Buehrle joked.

Pierzynski's shenanigans aren't limited to the ballfield. After the White Sox won the World Series in 2005, he made his debut as a professional wrestling manager on the Total Nonstop Action wrestling circuit. Pierzynski assumed the role of bad guy and even went at it with diminutive fan favorite, Big Leaguer David Eckstein. "I never get booed, so getting booed in the wrestling ring was really hard to take," Pierzynski cracked.

BOOMER

THE SAN DIEGO Padres' pitchers were taking part in routine drills during Spring Training in 2007 when one young ballplayer asked veteran hurler David Wells if he had a cough drop to spare. Happy to oblige, Wells pulled a lozenge from his back pocket and handed it to him.

As if on cue, Greg Maddux's sly deadpan pierced the morning silence.

"Do you have a candy bar in there, too?" said Maddux, eliciting chuckles all around.

Wells trumped that punchline when he arrived for stretching early the next day carrying a Baby Ruth bar. When it came to getting the last word — or the most enduring laugh — few players could win a one-on-one matchup with "Boomer."

Wells, who broke into the Major Leagues with Jimmy Key, Dave Stieb and the Toronto Blue Jays in 1987, retired in 2007 with 239 career victories, a perfect game, three All-Star Game appearances, two championship rings and a passel of Babe Ruth memorabilia.

While lots of players drift from playing baseball to managing hitting or pitching schools or opening car washes, Wells walked an alternate path. He packed his bow and arrow and went on an African safari, then traveled to Alaska to hunt bears.

Wells, whose playing weight hovered in the mid-200s for much of his career, also went to work as a baseball commentator for TBS. Basketball analyst Charles Barkley publicly approved the hire because he said the network now had an analyst who was "fatter" than him.

"He must have meant 'phat,'" Wells replied.

DID IT BOUNCE?

It was early in the Series, but a play in Game 2 proved to be a pivotal moment in the 2005 ALCS. With the Angels ahead in the Series, 1-0, and the score tied, 1-1, with two outs in the bottom of the ninth inning, the White Sox's A.J. Pierzynski swung at and missed strike three, but ran to first anyway. As the Angels returned to the dugout, home plate umpire Doug Eddings ruled that the ball hit the ground and was not fielded cleanly by Angels catcher Josh Paul, and Pierzynski was safe at first. "I didn't hear [Eddings] call me out, so I thought for sure the ball hit the ground," Pierzynski said after the game. "I watched the replay 50 times and still don't know."

Running for Pierzynski, Pablo Ozuna would score the winning run on a Joe Crede base hit, giving Chicago momentum as it won eight straight games to take the world title.

Fans around the league might have a love-hate relationship wtih Pierzynski, but no one doubts his smarts, especially after his heady play in Game 2 of the 2005 ALCS.

CHAPTER 7

WINNING COMBINATIONS

Minnesota Twins catcher Joe Mauer might be one of a kind, but he works even better in tandem. Early in his career, Mauer shared an apartment with fellow Twin Justin Morneau, and the teammates would talk baseball over lunch, at the park, and back and forth during the commute. The operative phrase is "synergy." Take a star-caliber player, complement him with an equally-skilled teammate who pushes him to greater heights, and it can spell double trouble for the opposition. Any pitcher forced to navigate this type of combination knows the feeling.

M&M BOYS

THE MINNESOTA TWINS have a proud and illustrious history of standout players — from Tony Oliva and Harmon Killebrew in the 1960s to Rod Carew and Kirby Puckett in subsequent decades. Starting in 2004, the Twins had the luxury of running out franchise faces in stereo. Catcher Joe Mauer, the All-American boy, and his Canadian counterpart, first baseman Justin Morneau, became as identifiable with Minnesota as any Twins before them.

They were dubbed the "M&M boys," for their initials, as the elite Yankees duo of Mickey Mantle and Roger Maris had been in the 1960s. Soft-spoken and hard-working, they were perfect for a franchise that values continuity and sound play. Aside from sharing an apartment and becoming friends away from the game, they fed off of one another on the field.

"He's very important to me as a hitter, because he gets on base so much and sees so many pitches," Morneau said of Mauer. "How he wears out pitchers, it makes a difference."

Mauer, a native of St. Paul, Minn., was a three-sport star at Cretin-Derham Hall High School, and skilled enough on the football field to merit a scholarship to Florida State to play quarterback. When the hometown Twins selected him first overall in the 2001 First-Year Player Draft — ahead of star pitcher Mark Prior — the choice was easy for Mauer.

Morneau, a product of New Westminster, B.C., was a standout baseball player and hockey goalie in his youth. The Twins selected him in the third round of the 1999 draft, and Morneau hit .310 in six seasons in the Minors before graduating to the Bigs.

Since teaming up, the M&M boys have shown a fondness for hardware. Mauer won two Silver Slugger Awards, made two All-Star teams and won a Gold Glove, all before his 26th birthday. Morneau won an MVP Award and two Silver Sluggers by age 27, and outlasted Josh Hamilton in the 2008 Home Run Derby.

Mauer (left) and Morneau, good friends off the field, made up a powerful offensive combo in the second half of the decade.

While Hall of Famers from Paul Molitor to Cal Ripken Jr. raved about Mauer's sweet left-handed swing, Morneau developed a reputation as the solid, reliable, RBI machine in the middle of the Twins' order. Together, they were good enough to coax an old Reggie Jackson line out of Minnesota Manager Ron Gardenhire.

"They are the straws that stir the drink in this lineup," Gardenhire said.

BEHIND THE SCENES

BOSTON MANAGER TERRY Francona doesn't need to listen to the chatter on sports talk radio and Internet fan blogs. More often than not, the scoreboard tells him all he needs to know about his public image.

When the Red Sox succeed, Francona is doing his job as well as any other Major League manager. But when the team fails, it's a given that somebody out there in Red Sox Nation will criticize him for a lack of judgment and foresight, and even attack his fundamental intelligence, mincing no words.

His boss, General Manager Theo Epstein, knows the feeling.

"Just ask the fans, and we're both bums or both great depending on whether we won or lost the day before," Epstein said.

But Red Sox fans, renowned for their passion, had little to complain about for most of the 2000s. After 86 titleless seasons, the Red Sox ended their alleged "Curse of the Bambino" with a world championship in 2004. The Sox and their fans enjoyed the experience so much, they did it again three years later.

Credit the GM and manager for helping to make it happen. Epstein — the youngest general manager in Major League history when he earned the title in 2002 at 28 years of age — displayed admirable intelligence and organizational savvy, and balanced a sense of urgency with the ability to think long-term. He also made a smart call when he hired Francona to fill the vacant managerial job in 2003.

"We knew that he would be extremely prepared and have sound baseball instincts and reasoning," Epstein said. "We saw a guy who would care about the players and treat them fairly, and have a good personal touch with all the different constituencies — media, fans, players, coaches and the front office. Luckily for us, he's proven us right on all those fronts, and then some."

FLAMETHROWERS

GREAT PITCHING COMBINATIONS are a rarity, but you know one when you see it. The possibilities seemed endless when Mark Prior and Kerry Wood were shutting down opposing lineups in tandem on Chicago's north side during the 2003 season.

Wood and Prior were the talk of the baseball scene that year. The young right-handers combined for a 32-17 record, including 511 strikeouts in 422.1 innings, and displayed the type of poise typically ascribed to veterans. Wood, the former 1998 Rookie of the Year, had electric stuff, scouts said, and Prior seemed so mechanically sound that it was hard to envision anything going wrong when he took the mound.

The pair pitched the Cubs to a National League Central title in 2003 and came within five outs of a pennant before Chicago suffered a seven-game loss to the Marlins in the NLCS.

But suddenly, and inexplicably, after that 2003 season ended, everything went wrong for the duo. Prior missed the first two months of 2004 with an Achilles injury and suffered a fractured elbow in 2005 when he was hit by a line drive off the bat of Colorado outfielder Brad Hawpe.

Previous spread: Epstein (left) and Francona worked together to turn the Red Sox from a title-starved team to a yearly threat. Opposite: Wood (center) made his first All-Star Game appearance with his partner in crime, Prior (far right), at the 2003 Midsummer Classic at U.S. Cellular Field in Chicago.

Wood missed two months himself with a strained triceps muscle in 2004, and later suffered injuries to his shoulder and knee. He even managed to take a spill getting out of a hot tub during Spring Training in 2007.

By the 2009 season, the 32-year-old Wood had relocated to Cleveland, serving as the Indians' new closer. Prior, meanwhile, attempted unsuccessfully to make a comeback in the Padres organization.

BROTHER ACT

THE COASTAL REGION of Virginia around Chesapeake and Virginia Beach has become known as a bountiful baseball talent source, with Michael Cuddyer, David Wright, Mark Reynolds and Ryan Zimmerman among the notable prodigies to graduate from area youth leagues to the Majors in recent years.

But one particular Chesapeake duo once slept under Manny and Yvonne Upton's roof.

Justin and B.J. Upton, baseball brothers with 10 tools in a single household, burst onto the scene via Major League Baseball's annual First-Year Player Draft. In 2002, Tampa Bay selected B.J. with the second overall pick. Three years later, the Arizona Diamondbacks chose Justin with the first overall pick.

"Sometimes when we're sitting at home, watching them on TV, I find myself trying to comprehend that I have two sons and they're both in the Major Leagues," Yvonne said. "I'll say to Manny, 'Can you believe this? Did you ever believe this was going to happen?' And we both have to say no."

Talent notwithstanding, the brothers took some lumps before ascending to star status in the pros. B.J. made 42 errors as a Class-A shortstop, and didn't establish himself as an everyday player in the Majors until the Rays moved him to center field in 2007.

Justin, the younger one, had a lot to learn after the Diamondbacks rushed him to the Big Leagues at age 19. He hit .221 in 43 games in his first call-up. But he showed all the signs of stardom by his third season in 2009, punctuated by his first All-Star Game appearance. "His future is definitely as bright as anyone's around," Diamondbacks Manager A.J. Hinch said. "There's nothing in this game he can't accomplish."

ALL-STAR SWAP

ALEX RODRIGUEZ grew up in Miami with a poster of Cal Ripken Jr. on his bedroom wall. In one of their few moments together on the national stage, A-Rod made a gesture that was equal parts poignant and symbolic. Rodriguez put his boyhood hero over his own ego at the 2001 All-Star Game when he swapped positions with Ripken, shifting from shortstop to third base so that the 19-time All-Star could take a final spin at the position that defined his Hall of Fame career. The move made plain the generational changing of the guard that was taking place.

Rodriguez ran the plan past American League Manager Joe Torre beforehand, but it clearly caught Ripken by surprise. Ripken initially seemed reluctant to move, then agreed to change positions with Rodriguez to the delight of the 47,364 fans in Seattle. The swap lasted one inning.

The gesture helped win over the crowd at Seattle's Safeco Field, which had been hostile in its treatment of Rodriguez since he had left the Mariners to sign a 10-year, $252 million contract with the Texas Rangers less than a year earlier.

"When I thought about it more, it was a really neat tribute," Ripken said.

Ripken, appropriately, homered off the Dodgers' Chan Ho Park to lead the American League to a 4-1 victory. He capped his 18th All-Star Game appearance with his second career Midsummer Classic MVP Award.

"All I could think of was Ted Williams hitting a home run in his final at-bat in the Major Leagues," said Arizona pitcher Curt Schilling, a former Ripken teammate in Baltimore.

BIG APPLE BIG SHOTS

IN THE SPAN of a week in late November 2005, the New York Mets acquired slugging first baseman Carlos Delgado from the Florida Marlins by trade and signed free-agent closer Billy Wagner. But when the organization released its ticket schedule to fans over the winter, the cover photo featured a smiling Jose Reyes exchanging a high-five with his buddy, David Wright.

Opposite: Rodriguez switched places with Ripken (left) during the 2001 All-Star Game in Seattle. Next spread: Mets infielders Wright (left) and Reyes have been a solid infield tandem and leaders for New York.

"I think the fans connect with the younger guys," General Manager Omar Minaya said. "They know that, in t[he] age of free agency, these guys are going to be around for the next four or five years. That's the goal."

Although Minaya would go on to face a multitude of personnel challenges in other areas during the next few se[a]sons, he could rest assured that stability wouldn't be a problem on the left side of the infield.

Wright, a policeman's son from Virginia, made his first All-Star team at age 23 and added a Gold Glove and a Sil[ver] Slugger Award a year later. In 2007, he joined Howard Johnson and Darryl Strawberry as the third Met in the 30-ho[me] run, 30-steal club.

Reyes signed with New York out of a camp in his native Dominican Republic, but endured growing pains before beco[m]ing an All-Star at age 23. He suffered from leg injuries early in his career, and briefly moved to second base to accommod[ate] Japanese import Kaz Matsui.

While both players took some grief after the Mets missed the playoffs in the latter part of the decade, they remain[ed] dedicated to bringing a winner to New York.

"I want to be here, and I want to win a championship here," Wright said. "And if anyone wants to lay blame for w[hat] has happened to us, they should blame me. I want that responsibility. I want to be that kind of player. Me and Jose[,] think we both want that."

DIAMOND ARMS

WHEN ALL IS said and done, Randy Johnson will be remembered for his blistering fastball, his "Mr. Snappy" slid[er,] his wild mullet and his menacing scowl. Curt Schilling's calling cards were his loquaciousness, his flair for clutch performances in big games, and his "bloody sock" heroics of the 2004 postseason.

Johnson is a Hall of Fame lock with more than 300 career victories, and Schilling will possibly make it to Cooperstown as well, so their individual exploits are undeniable. But for a brief time in the early 2000s, it was impossible to mention one without the other.

RANDY JOHNSON'S AND CURT SCHILLING'S STATS FROM 2001–02					
JOHNSON					
ERA	IP	W-L	BB	K	WHIP
2.40	509.2	45-11	142	706	1.02
SCHILLING					
ERA	IP	W-L	BB	K	WHIP
3.10	516.0	45-13	72	609	1.08

During two transcendent seasons with Arizona in 2001 and 2002, Johnson and Schilling staged perhaps the most awesome display of pitching ever seen by a [two-man] combination. The pair elicited comparisons to Sandy Koufax and Don Drysdale, Warren Spahn and Johnny Sain, G[reg] Maddux and Tom Glavine, some of the greatest top-of-the-rotation tandems in baseball history.

The numbers were staggering: Johnson and Schilling posted a combined 90-24 record and averaged 11.54 stri[ke]outs per nine innings during those two seasons. Johnson won back-to-back Cy Young Awards, while Schilling finish[ed] second in the balloting both years.

Their brilliance was particularly evident during the 2001 postseason, when they combined for a 9-1 record and a 1.31 E[RA] on the way to the Diamondbacks' first world championship. Fittingly enough, they shared the World Series MVP Award, as [the] Diamondbacks outlasted the Yankees in seven games. Later that year, *Sports Illustrated* named them Sportsmen of the Year.

"A lot of people said you can't win with just two pitchers," said Arizona General Manager Joe Garagiola Jr. "I thi[nk] it depends on which two you get."

BIG THREE BREAK UP

GREG MADDUX, TOM GLAVINE and John Smoltz spent their first decade in the Major Leagues applying the stamp [of] greatness to their careers. In the second decade, they perfected the whole longevity thing. The contingent known as [the] "Big Three" attained some major milestones in the 2000s. Maddux and Glavine joined the 300-win club, and Sm[oltz] became the first pitcher in history to accumulate 200 victories and 150 saves.

Their last season as a threesome in Atlanta came in 2002. Glavine signed as a free agent with the New York M[ets] the following winter, and Maddux left for the Chicago Cubs in 2004. Although Glavine and Smoltz reunited w[ith]

Johnson (left) and Schilling were co-MVPs of the 2001 World Series.

96

the Braves in 2008, Maddux spent his twilight years on the West Coast in Los Angeles and San Diego.

Maddux was the professorial one; Glavine the tough, resourceful lefty; and Smoltz the guy with the power package that hitters dreaded facing. The final tally for the Big Three from 1993–2002: five Cy Young Awards, nine division titles, three National League pennants and a World Series victory over Cleveland in 1995.

"We witnessed something very special here for those years they were together," Braves President John Schuerholz said. "So special that it's hard to imagine it happening again."

As great as the three pitchers were, they fed off each other and made each other better. More important, they made winning contagious in Atlanta.

By 2009, Maddux had retired, Smoltz was pitching in Boston, and Glavine was home with his family after a comeback attempt sputtered.

"I was in the midst of greatness, and I enjoyed every bit that those 10 years provided," Smoltz said. "Not to mention I beat them in golf every time that I played with them, so that was fun, too."

TWICE AS NICE

IT PAYS TO be a switch-hitter when, for instance, left-hander Randy Johnson is staring in for the sign and readying his slider grip. John Kruk's priceless strikeout against Johnson from the left side of the plate in the 1993 All-Star Game said everything that needed to be said about the value of hitting from both sides.

But no one ever said it was easy.

"It takes twice as long to prepare and twice as many swings," said Yankees first baseman Mark Teixeira. "Sometimes you can drive yourself crazy trying to keep *two* swings right."

When Teixeira and fellow switch-hitters Chipper Jones and Lance Berkman are truly in sync, pitchers suffer a lot more than the batters do and a lot more than Kruk did. Three of the most productive switch-hitters in baseball history spent the decade demoralizing pitching rotations from East coast to West coast. On Aug. 26, 2006, Jones, the long-time face of the Atlanta Braves, moved into third place on the list of career home runs by a switch-hitter, in good company, behind Mickey Mantle and Eddie Murray. Teixeira, meanwhile, hit 203 home runs in his first six Major League seasons, the most ever by a switch-hitter in that time span. And Berkman, Houston's self-described "Big Puma," joined Jones, Mantle and Murray as the only members of the fraternity to hit 25 or more home runs in seven campaigns.

"When I started switch-hitting, no way in a million years would I have ever thought that I would be hitting 400 homers in the Major Leagues," Jones said. "I was thinking: Steal 30 bases a year, slap the ball and hit .300 from both sides of the plate."

Throw Victor Martinez, Carlos Beltran and Jimmy Rollins into the mix, and the 2000s looked a lot like a golden age for switch-hitters. If Teixeira thinks life is challenging for him and his fellow switch-hitting batsmen, he should try to imagine how opposing managers feel when handling their bullpens against them.

Teixeira and his fellow All-Star switch-hitters can wreak havoc on opposing pitchers and managers' bullpen strategies.

WHEN TEIXEIRA AND FELLOW SWITCH-HITTERS CHIPPER JONES AND LANCE BERKMAN ARE TRULY IN SYNC, PITCHERS SUFFER A LOT MORE THAN THE BATTERS DO.

CHAPTER 8

YOUTH

Nothing trumps experience on the field — except maybe fresh legs, quick wrists and youthful exuberance. Longtime Manager Jim Leyland lives by the mantra, "Give me talent over experience any day," and there was no shortage of young talent in the 2000s. Albert Pujols was 21 years old when he hit .329 with 37 homers in 2001. Think he required more seasoning? At the end of the decade, Arizona's 21-year-old Justin Upton earned raves for hitting moon shots and covering the gaps with ease. The only thing more impressive than Upton's raw skills was his potential.

WORLD CLASS

WHILE COLUMNISTS AND radio and TV commentators hashed over his decision to start 24-year-old Josh Beckett on three days' rest in Game 6 of the 2003 World Series — amid the daunting backdrop of Yankee Stadium, no less — Florida Marlins Manager Jack McKeon had no doubt that he was making the correct call.

"If I had Bob Gibson out there on three days' rest, would anybody ask why I wanted to pitch him?" McKeon asked. "No. And that's how we feel about Josh Beckett."

After the Marlins beat the Yankees, 2-0, for their second title in seven years, Beckett packed up his World Series MVP trophy and went home to Texas for some deer hunting. And McKeon was free to say "I told you so" to the national media.

"I guess you'll believe me now," McKeon said. "This guy is special. You all kept asking me why I'd start him on three days' rest. Now you know."

Beckett, the second pick in the 1999 First-Year Player Draft, had been preparing all his life for this grand stage. He grew up in Spring, Texas, and fit the mold of the hard-throwing right-hander personified by fellow Texans Nolan Ryan and Roger Clemens. Self-assuredness certainly wasn't a problem; upon signing with the Marlins in 1999, Beckett himself predicted that he would be pitching in the All-Star Game by 2001.

In the summer of 2003, Beckett combined with fellow youngsters Brad Penny, Carl Pavano, Mark Redman and Dontrelle Willis to pitch the Marlins to 91 victories, a Wild Card berth and playoff wins over the Giants and Cubs. The Florida starters ranged in age from 21 (Willis) to 29 (Redman).

Beckett pitched well in a 6-1 defeat at the hands of New York in Game 3 of the World Series in Florida, and he never hesitated to take the ball on three days' rest for the pivotal

Beckett celebrates after tagging the Yankees' Jorge Posada for the World Series–clinching out in 2003.

101

...me 6. After he struck out nine batters and held the powerful Yankees lineup to five hits and two walks in the clincher, ...was easy to see why.

The headstrong Beckett had grown accustomed to people calling him "cocky." Now, along with remaining detractors, he ...d to get acclimated to the idea of being a world champion.

"I can't believe we don't have a game tomorrow," Beckett said after the Series-clinching game. "Not to say that winning ...e world championship isn't a big thing. It's kind of a relief to get to go deer hunting now."

...HE FREAK

...N FRANCISCO GIANTS starter Tim Lincecum posted an 18-5 record in 2008 for a team that finished 72-90. He led the ...ajor Leagues with 265 strikeouts and joined Fernando Valenzuela and Vida Blue on the short list of pitchers to win a Cy ...ung Award in their first full Big League season.

Lincecum's 5'11", 170-pound physique, downy cheeks and youthful countenance belie an imposing presence when he's ...nding on the mound. He throws a two-seam fastball in the upper 90s, a formidable change-up and a curveball with an ...orthodox delivery that prevents hitters from picking up the ball until it's far too late.

"He looks like one of the Jonas Brothers," said San Francisco teammate Randy Johnson.

At age 24, Lincecum joined Mike McCormick of the 1967 Giants as only the second San Francisco pitcher to capture ...Cy Young Award.

Lincecum's breakthrough season led to a busy winter of appearances and endorsements. He dropped the ceremonial ...st puck at a San Jose Sharks hockey game, starred in a commercial for a popular video game, and took some bows while ...ending a basketball game at his old school, the University of Washington. The following season he was chosen to start for ...e NL in the All-Star Game. Still, no one expected the modest, fun-loving Lincecum to let the attention go to his head.

"I'm the same person," Lincecum emphasized. "The only difference is that I have a little hardware now."

...ARLY RISER

...VAN LONGORIA BECAME a Tampa Bay Ray, a wealthy young man and a Major League All-...ar all between April and July 2008. Then the second half of the season began and Longoria ...ctured his wrist, endured a strenuous rehab to return to the field, played in the World Series ...d won the American League Rookie of the Year Award. It's hard to imagine cramming more ...to a six-month stretch, especially at the age of 22.

But Longoria navigated the highs and lows with a maturity beyond his years, possessing a ...re mix of leadership and talent that prompts veteran players to hold him in high esteem, even ...ough he's just a few years removed from his senior prom.

"I hear guys saying, 'Man, he's got an unbelievable approach at the plate, the way he ex-...odes his hips and his bat stays in the zone for such a long time,'" said Tampa Bay pitcher ...mes Shields. "It's amazing. This guy is 22 years old, and other guys want to be like him."

Tampa Bay Senior Baseball Advisor Don Zimmer has compared Longoria favorably to ...ike Schmidt, Brooks Robinson and all the other elite third basemen he has seen play since ...eaking into the Majors in 1954. The Rays were so sufficiently sold on Longoria's future that ...ey signed him to a lucrative six-year deal in April 2008 after he had appeared in a total of ...x Big League games.

ALCS HERO

During the 2008 American League Championship Series, Rays third baseman Evan Longoria, like the young franchise for which he played, had neither age nor experience — but that didn't seem to affect his contributions to the team. At just 22 — and without a full year of Major League service under his belt — Longoria was the force that propelled Tampa Bay to its first-ever postseason. And not satisfied simply to be there, he also propelled the Rays to the Fall Classic.

In seven ALCS games against the defending champion Boston Red Sox, the slugging right-hander launched four home runs — one each in Games 2-5 — and his bat provided the Rays with the RBI that tied the final game of the Series, ultimately leading Tampa Bay to the World Series.

...ADIES' MAN

...HE WOMEN IN charge of the Grady's Ladies Sisterhood are only too happy to spread the word on behalf of the Cleveland ...dians' quiet superstar, Grady Sizemore.

"Our favorite player might not care too much for talkin' about himself (he lets his sweet five-tool skill set do the talking ...r him, you see) but we'll chat him up tons," the group says on its website.

Opposite: Lincecum has become one of the most feared pitchers in the Bigs. Next spread: Longoria quickly ascended to stardom as a rookie.

True, Sizemore isn't much for self promotion. But thanks to his three All-Star Game appearances, two Gold Gloves a four 100-run seasons by age 26, he established himself as a civic treasure in Cleveland.

An all-around star athlete in high school, Sizemore turned down a football scholarship to play quarterback for the U versity of Washington to sign with the Montreal Expos. The Indians acquired Sizemore, Cliff Lee and Brandon Phillips pitcher Bartolo Colon in a one-sided trade with the Expos in June 2002.

While Sizemore's good looks have made him a favorite with Cleveland's female fans, old-school baseball people preciate him for his intensity and passion for the game. Sizemore's love of baseball shows through his desire to play ev day and improve upon his weaknesses with hard work. He has also displayed a willingness to sacrifice his body to cat anything close to him in the outfield.

"If I was going to start a team today, I'd start with Grady Sizemore," said former Big League All-Star and Manag Buddy Bell. "I love the way that kid plays."

THE NATURAL

HANLEY RAMIREZ DEVELOPED a nice little synergy with his teammates in his first four seasons as a Florida Marlin: Wh he was winning games and collecting plaudits, his teammates were stockpiling stories. Just about everyone in the Flori clubhouse has a tale of a wondrous athletic feat by Ramirez — and they don't all involve baseball skills.

During Spring Training in 2009, Marlins catcher John Baker told a reporter about the time Ramirez, a talented bask ball player as a youth in the Dominican Republic, wagered that he could shoot a baseball from his shortstop position ir a bucket of balls located next to first base.

"I said, 'Sure, Hanley,'" Baker recalled. "So with perfect basketball shooting form, like a free throw, or little jumper, shot a baseball from shortstop into the bucket. I threw up my hands and said, 'That's it — I quit.'"

Ramirez, regarded as an unpolished but extremely talented prospect in the Boston Red Sox's farm system, blossom into a superstar after coming to Florida by trade in November 2005 — a deal that landed ace Josh Beckett in Bostc benefiting both sides. Ramirez displayed a rare blend of speed, power and durability while playing one of the game's m demanding positions.

"Hanley Ramirez is in a class of his own," said second baseman Dan Uggla, Ramirez's double-play partner in Florid

Ramirez won the Rookie of the Year Award at age 22, ranked 10th in MVP balloting at 23, and led the National Leag with 125 runs scored at 24.

In the spring of 2009, *The Sporting News* surveyed 100 Hall of Famers and other former Major Leaguers and ask them to rank the 50 greatest active players in the game. The panel ranked Ramirez fifth behind Albert Pujols, Alex Rod guez, Johan Santana and Manny Ramirez. At age 25, Hanley Ramirez was the youngest player to crack the top 10.

KING FELIX

WHEN YOU'VE APPEARED on national magazine covers and been anointed a franchise's savior as a teenager, it's not ea to take a step back and a corresponding deep breath. Few ballplayers understand that better than Felix Hernandez, w arrived in Seattle at age 19 in the summer of 2005 amid breathless expectations.

The Seattle fan base referred to Hernandez as "King Felix." Some scouts compared him to a young Dwight Goodc and *Baseball America* called him "unquestionably the best pitching prospect in baseball."

In August 2005, the 19-year-old Hernandez made his first Big League start against Detroit. He was the young pitcher to make his debut in a starting role since Britt Burns of the Chicago White Sox in 1978.

Hernandez pitched solidly in a 3-1 loss, and finished the season with a 4-4 record and a 2.67 ERA. In hindsight, admitted, the early buildup was a bit suffocating.

"It got to be too much," Hernandez said. "I got a little overwhelmed with it."

Although Hernandez experienced some ups and downs in the ensuing years, he also showed signs of maturity. ranked among the top 10 in the American League in strikeouts each year from 2006–08, posted a 14-7 record in 200 pitched 200 innings for the first time in 2008 and made his first All-Star team in 2009.

It remained to be seen if he would live up to the early "King" talk. But he clearly showed that he belonged.

CHAPTER 9
GREAT CLOSERS

Some skeptics contend that the save is an overrated statistic, and that closers are beneficiaries of excessive hype. To which we reply: Try being a legitimate contender without one. The elite closers — Mariano Rivera, Trevor Hoffman, Jonathan Papelbon, Joe Nathan and company — give their managers a sense of security and fans a nice, warm feeling when the bullpen door swings open in the ninth inning. They have knockout stuff, short memories, personal anthems and a fondness for exchanging high-fives with teammates at the end of their outings.

SAVE THE MOMENT

FOR MOST OF his career, Trevor Hoffman stockpiled his signature statistic around 10 p.m. PDT — a time when jewel thieves, infomercial hosts and 7-Eleven clerks did their best work on the East Coast. It was around this time on June 6, 2007, that Hoffman froze Dodgers catcher Russell Martin with a fastball to preserve a 5-2 San Diego victory and become the first reliever to reach 500 career saves. While much of the nation was asleep, the moment was cause for reverie at Petco Park in San Diego.

Teammates David Wells and Mike Cameron lifted Hoffman onto their shoulders and carried him across the infield, and Greg Maddux, who logged his 338th victory the night of Hoffman's 500th save, sounded grateful to be part of the special event.

"It's cool," Maddux said. "I had a chance to witness history. The guy's doing something nobody in baseball has ever done. For me personally, I felt privileged to see it."

Hoffman has done his job so deftly for so long, it's easy to forget the long road he traveled. He broke into professional baseball as a shortstop in the Reds organization, and his time seemed to be running out after he hit .212 with myriad errors for Class-A Charleston in 1990. That's when Jim Lett, his manager, decided to convert him to a pitcher.

"He was a good enough athlete, and the ball came out of his hand so easy," Lett said. "With his arm strength we figured, 'What do we have to lose?' But who would have ever thought this would happen? It was like winning the lottery."

Hoffman's career path carried him from Cincinnati to Florida to San Diego, where he stuck around long enough to inherit the "face of the franchise" designation from Hall of Famer Tony Gwynn. When his radar gun readings declined because of a shoulder injury, he continued to thrive on the strength of one of baseball's best change-ups.

Hoffman was carried off the field by Padres teammates in June 2007 after he became the first closer in Big League history to notch 500 career saves.

"If you watch video of Trevor and slow it down, you'd think his change-up was a knuckleball," said Padres reliever Doug Bocail. "It's there and gone. See ya. Bye."

Hoffman officially said goodbye to San Diego in January 2009, when he signed with the Milwaukee Brewers as a free agent. By that point, he had long since signed, sealed and delivered his induction into Cooperstown.

GAME OVER

THE LAW OF averages says that no matter how well a closer throws, he's going to blow a save now and then through a combination of unforeseen circumstances or simple bad luck. A ground ball will go through the shortstop's legs. A broken bat blooper will land in the middle of three fielders. The sun will get in somebody's eyes.

The folks in charge apparently forgot to mention that section of the baseball bylaws to Eric Gagne.

During a remarkable run with the Dodgers from 2002–04, including a Cy Young Award in 2003, Gagne averaged 13.3 strikeouts and 2.1 walks for every nine innings, converting 152 of 158 save chances. Gagne also fueled a run on his "Game Over" T-shirts by converting a record 84 save chances in a row from Aug. 26, 2002, to July 5, 2004. He obliterated the previous record of 54, held by Tom Gordon.

ERIC GAGNE'S 2003 STATS								
ERA	IP	W-L	BB	K	SV	BS	K/BB	WHIP
1.20	82.1	2-3	20	137	55	0	6.85	0.692

Then-Dodgers Manager Jim Tracy compared Gagne's save streak to Joe DiMaggio's 56-game hit streak, Ted Williams' .406 average in 1941, Cal Ripken Jr.'s 2,632 consecutive games played and Orel Hershiser's 59 scoreless innings in the ranks of monumental achievements.

"I've said this a few times — I don't know if you or I or anybody else in our lifetime will see a streak like this," Tracy said.

THE SANDMAN

CASUAL NEW YORK baseball fans may have thought something was amiss on Opening Day 2006 when Billy Wagner, the new Mets closer, jogged out of the Shea Stadium bullpen to the accompaniment of "Enter Sandman." Many felt that

Opposite: Rivera picked up where he left off in the '90s, remaining the best closer in the game. This page: Gagne pumps his fist after locking down another save in 2004 during his historic streak.

Mariano Rivera — who recorded his 500th save on June 28, 2009, and is widely considered the greatest closer of all time — was the rightful owner of that entrance music.

The dispute was no big deal for Wagner, who actually used the song first.

"I play for the Mets. Mariano plays for the Yankees," Wagner said. "I never have to face him and he never has to face me, so there's no big competition there. The earth isn't going to crumble just because two guys have it."

But a die-hard Yankees fan knows that there is only one Sandman.

Rivera, arguably the best money closer in history, maintained his record of excellence through a new decade, overpowering hitters with his trademark cut fastball even as he approached age 40. On Sept. 15, 2008, he closed out the Chicago White Sox, 4-2, to register his 479th save and pass Lee Smith to move into second place behind Trevor Hoffman on the career list. Rivera struck out 77 batters, walked just six and limited opposing hitters to a .165 batting average in 2008 — arguably the finest season of his stellar career — even while pitching in constant discomfort. He underwent surgery shortly after the season to repair the AC joint in his right shoulder.

"I think Mariano is the best closer ever, there's no doubt about that," said catcher Jorge Posada. "So persistent, the longevity of it."

He won't get any argument from Yankees fans on that one.

HEAVEN SENT

ANGELS MANAGER MIKE Scioscia sensed his team might be onto something special in the fall of 2002, when right-handed reliever Francisco Rodriguez arrived from Triple-A and fit in so seamlessly as Troy Percival's main set-up man. The precocious kid — called "K-Rod" for his propensity to strike out opposing batters — posted a 5-1 record in the postseason; struck out 28 Yankees, Twins and Giants in 18.2 innings; and set an unofficial record for wrenched backs and disheartened expressions by opposing hitters.

"It took about three appearances before we knew he'd be part of things if we made the playoffs," Scioscia said. "And it took about two outings in the playoffs before we said, 'You know what, this kid is going to pitch deep in the game before Percival.' He wasn't scared and his stuff was electric."

How good did the kid turn out to be? Record-setting good.

Rodriguez made history during the 2008 season when he saved 62 games to break Bobby Thigpen's 18-year-old record of 57. Rodriguez posted No. 58 on Sept. 13, striking out Raul Ibanez to seal a 5-2 victory over Seattle.

Rodriguez relied on a low-90s fastball, a tight curve and an effective change-up to set the record. He told reporters that he felt the presence of his grandfather — who had been a major source of support when he was growing up amid poverty in his native Venezuela and died in April 1999.

RODRIGUEZ MADE HISTORY DURING THE 2008 SEASON WHEN HE SAVED 62 GAMES TO BREAK BOBBY THIGPEN'S 18-YEAR-OLD RECORD OF 57.

Rodriguez rejoices after his record-tying 57th save in 2008. Two days later he became the single-season saves leader in Major League history.

"I felt like he was right next to me," Rodriguez said. "He's with me every day. I would give up anything to have h right next to me and enjoy this moment."

LIGHTS OUT

AT THE 2007 GM meetings in Orlando, the Phillies acquired a closer with a surgically repaired right knee and a seemingly fragile ego. But the glowing scouting reports and Brad Lidge's impressive 11.82 strikeouts per nine innings with Houston during the previous seas told the Philadelphia front office all it needed to know about the former All-Star reliever.

BRAD LIDGE'S 2008 STATS								
ERA	IP	W-L	BB	K	SV	BS	K/BB	WHIP
1.95	69.1	2-0	35	92	41	0	2.63	1.226

"At the end of the year, our scouts saw him throwing the ball as well as he's ever thrown it," said Ruben Amaro J then the Phillies' assistant GM. "Based on his pedigree and his history, that's good enough for us. He's still what would consider a premier closer."

This is known in the business as an "understatement."

Lidge, invigorated by his new surroundings and the challenge of a pennant race, was lights out for the Phillies 2008, even managing the tightrope that every hurler must walk in cozy Citizens Bank Park. After he converted his fi 19 save opportunities, the Phillies rewarded him with a three-year contract extension in July.

Lidge converted his last 22 save opportunities to make it 41 straight in the regular season, then posted a 0.96 EF in October. He dropped to his knees in celebration after striking out Tampa Bay's Eric Hinske for the final out of t World Series, and was embraced by catcher Carlos Ruiz.

"I always figured I'd be jumping up and down, but I guess it happened and that's how I felt," Lidge said. "I said, 'C my God, we just won the World Series.'"

Lidge came back to earth in the early part of 2009, missing time in Spring Training with forearm tightness, a blowing his first regular-season save in 48 chances in an April loss to San Diego. But the World Series video and th championship ring serve as indelible reminders of an untouchable season.

GETTING THE CALL

HALL OF FAMER Robin Yount didn't experience failure against many pitchers while amassing 3,142 career hits. But 6-for-37 career effort against Goose Gossage produced some rare moments of discomfort in the batter's box.

"If the game was on the line, you knew he was going to throw you fastballs, and every one got harder," Yount sai "And more smoke came out of his ears, and more stuff came out of his mouth. He was just grunting like a wild b out there, ready to charge."

Gossage's route to the Hall of Fame was not as direct as one of his blistering fastballs. It was more of a leisure stroll. The nine-time All-Star, who received Most Valuable Player and Cy Young votes in five different seasons an spent nine years on the Hall of Fame ballot, wasn't shy about giving history lessons to baseball writers who were hes tant to embrace his candidacy. But Gossage's discontent melted away when he delivered his speech at Cooperstow in July 2008.

"All I ever wanted to do was put on a Big League uniform for one day," Gossage told the assembled crowd. "That o time turned into 22 years. I just can't comprehend that. I still have to pinch myself that I had that kind of career."

Much to Gossage's chagrin, baseball writers have found it challenging in the past to assess the value of closers, b there were signs of a thaw this decade. In 2004, Dennis Eckersley received 84.7 percent of the vote to make it in Cooperstown as a first-ballot inductee. Although "Eck" was a 20-game winner as a starter early in his career, he ha more success later on when he became a lights-out reliever for the Oakland A's, pitching almost exclusively in the nin inning. Two years after Eckersley got the nod from the baseball writers, another late-game specialist got the call. Bru Sutter, father of the split-finger fastball, closed the deal in 2006 in his 13th appearance on the ballot.

Sutter, always in control on the mound, admitted that he cried upon hearing the news of his induction.

"It was the call you always hope for, but you never really expect it to happen," he said. "I didn't think it would affe me or hit me as hard as it did."

CHAPTER 10

SURPRISE SQUADS

Sure, a large payroll and steady revenue stream can give a franchise the luxury of papering over mistakes while still contending year in and year out. But dollars alone can't replace imagination and long-term vision. What makes the Florida Marlins so resilient, or the Minnesota Twins so consistently competitive? Some of these under-the-radar teams have success because of scouting acumen, while others are adept at analyzing numbers, but no matter what, they're all willing to explore every possible angle and think outside the box. Major League Baseball's subtle winners prove that the biggest Hot Stove headlines don't always lead to the final World Series celebration in October.

HOW THE WEST WAS WON

SAYING GOODBYE TO a Hall of Fame–caliber player is never easy. During an arduous stretch from 1998–2001, the Seattle Mariners made such farewells a habit. Baseball fans in the Pacific Northwest were disheartened after the Mariners traded pitcher Randy Johnson to Houston, sent outfielder Ken Griffey Jr. to Cincinnati and lost shortstop Alex Rodriguez to Texas through free agency during a two-and-a-half year stretch. Seattle began the 2001 season with Major League Baseball's 11th highest payroll, and most experts picked the Mariners to finish second or third in the American League West.

So much for the allure of "star power."

The Mariners dispelled the doubts about their talent, and made history along the way. They got off to a 20-5 start the first month and went on to post an overall record of 116-46, finishing 14 games ahead of a strong Oakland A's team. Seattle's win total tied the 1906 Chicago Cubs for most victories in a season. The Mariners lost, 4-3, to Texas on the final day of the season to fall one win short of breaking the record.

An incredibly balanced squad, the Mariners led the league in runs, batting average, stolen bases, ERA and fielding percentage. The only sour note to the feast was the final course. After beating Cleveland in the first round of the playoffs, Seattle lost to the Yankees in five games in the American League Championship Series. Although a rash of injuries didn't help Seattle's cause, the club played poorly against New York and dropped the series finale, 12-3.

Still, the Mariners' incredible regular season scored a haul of postseason awards. Lou Piniella won AL Manager of the Year. Japanese import Ichiro Suzuki pulled off a rare double by winning both the Most Valuable Player and Rookie of the Year awards, and second baseman Bret Boone finished third in MVP balloting on the strength of 37 homers and 141 RBI.

Ichiro gets high-fives after a May 3, 2001, win in Seattle, the M's 10th straight home victory and one of 57 home wins that year.

Pitcher Jamie Moyer recorded his first 20-win season that year at age 38, and Freddy Garcia, Paul Abbott and Aaron Sele won 15 games or more. Closer Kazuhiro Sazaki saved 45 contests in a strong follow-up to his Rookie of the Year season.

Despite the silence in the clubhouse following their season-ending loss to New York, the Mariners didn't focus on the negative, instead taking pride in accomplishing so much amid widespread skepticism.

"Those 116 wins are in the books," said outfielder Mike Cameron. "We played damn good baseball. That's what I going to remember."

THE RAYS SHINE

THE 2008 FALL Classic was cause for euphoria in Philadelphia, where fans hit the streets after the Phillies' Series-clinching Game 5 win to celebrate the city's first major sports championship in 25 years. But the end result, although a disappointment for the Tampa Bay Rays, couldn't obscure how far the franchise had come.

After nine last-place finishes in 10 years, the expansion Rays literally forged a new identity in 2008 by dropping "Devil" from their nickname and redesigning their uniforms and logos. And on the diamond, homegrown talents Evan Longoria, Carl Crawford and B.J. Upton matured in time to make the Rays a team to reckon with in the tough AL East.

Behind the steady, cerebral leadership of Manager Joe Maddon, the Rays overcame Major League Baseball's second-lowest payroll to go 97-65 and capture the franchise's first division title. They beat the White Sox and then the Red Sox in the first two rounds of the postseason before falling to Philadelphia in five games in the World Series.

At the peak of this team's grand adventure, cowbells clanged at Tropicana Field in St. Petersburg, "Rayhawk" haircuts became fashionable, and Rays fans Dick Vitale, Paul Azinger and Gen. David Petraeus were among the luminaries to throw out ceremonial first pitches.

"In the minds of a lot of people, just making it into the playoffs was a big thing for us," Longoria said. "Just winning 2 games was a big deal for this franchise. Obviously there's a great deal of disappointment that we didn't win the world championship. But when I go home and sit on my couch for a little bit, there's a lot more good than bad that happened this year."

MONEYBALL

THE SUREST WAY to start a spirited conversation in the spring of 2003 was to express an opinion on *Moneyball*, the national bestseller written by Michael Lewis. The book shed light on the inner workings of the Oakland front office and revealed how the Athletics used statistical analysis to exploit inefficiencies in the market for Big League players. The A's averaged nearly 94 wins a season between 1999 and 2006 with one of the lowest payrolls in the Majors. Although they never won the world title, they appeared in the postseason five times during that period.

The book also detailed the rise of Sabermetrics, profiling Bill James and other trailblazers in the field. But the undisputed star was A's General Manager Billy Beane, a former "can't miss" outfield prospect who washed out at the age of 27 because of an inability to hit Major League–caliber pitching. In his first five years as A's GM, Beane developed reputation as a smart guy with a flair for progressive thinking. But he attained a new level of fame in 2003, when he became a pop culture phenomenon.

Beane seemed amused by the perception in a select few quarters that he — not Lewis — had actually written *Moneyball*. He also did his best to dodge the hard feelings that divided scouts and statisticians in response to the book.

"I find it humorous that there's this sort of chasm between 'baseball people' and 'stat guys' or 'eggheads,'" Beane said. "People spend so much time trying to figure out which camp you're in. When you really sort of examine everybody's background, who cares?"

MILE-HIGH MIRACLE

THE COLORADO ROCKIES set an attendance record when they debuted in 1993, and the young franchise, buoyed by rabid fanbase, reached the playoffs two years later. Andres Galarraga, Dante Bichette and the "Blake Street Bombers" put up numbers in abundance, and the games in Denver were almost always entertaining — especially if you're partial to 12-11 contests. But for most of the 2000s, the Rockies stayed below the radar at 5,280 feet. The franchise's inability to develop

Longoria, Tampa Bay's rookie third baseman, celebrates after clinching the club's 2008 playoff berth at Tropicana Field, where the Rays beat the Twins, 7-2.

pitching was a perennial problem, and a $172.5 million expenditure on free-agent pitchers Mike Hampton and Denny Neagle in 2000 didn't help the cause.

The Rockies endured six straight sub-.500 seasons and seemed headed for another idle October in 2007 when things suddenly clicked. Behind the hitting of outfielder Matt Holliday, the stellar defense of rookie shortstop Troy Tulowitzki and a newfound sense of destiny, the Rockies simply refused to lose.

Colorado won 14 of its last 15 regular-season games and beat San Diego in a thrilling back-and-forth one-game playoff for the NL Wild Card berth. Then the Rockies swept Philadelphia and Arizona in seven straight playoff games to capture the franchise's first pennant. Although Boston's World Series sweep wasn't the ending the Rockies had in mind, the ride sure was fun while it lasted.

"When I see the pictures, I will remember what a special time this was," said first baseman Todd Helton. "For a bunch of regular guys, we accomplished a lot. I hope the city is proud of us, because I know I am."

> "I WILL REMEMBER WHAT A SPECIAL TIME THIS WAS. FOR A BUNCH OF REGULAR GUYS, WE ACCOMPLISHED A LOT. I HOPE THE CITY IS PROUD OF US." TODD HELTON

ALL IN THE FAMILY

THE MINNESOTA TWINS place a premium on accountability and loyalty — values that help maintain order even when a low budget puts a crimp in the organizational game plan.

The Twins made the playoffs from 2002–04, as well as in 2006, thanks to homegrown talent such as fan-favorite Torii Hunter, Cy Young winner Johan Santana and closer Joe Nathan. And they endured — still contending in the division — after losing Hunter to the Angels through free agency and after trading Santana to the Mets for four prospects once it became apparent they weren't going to be able to sign him to a long-term deal. In addition, the Twins overcame the surprise retirement of General Manager Terry Ryan, an ace talent evaluator who took over in 1994 and whose name appeared regularly at the top of "best front office executive" lists.

Bill Smith, who succeeded Ryan in 2007, cites continuity throughout the organization as a major factor in the Twins' success throughout the decade. Mike Radcliff, who took over as the Twins' scouting director in 1993, is still scoping out talent from all over as the team's vice president of player personnel, and Minnesota's Minor League instructors teach the fundamentals the same way at every stop. Since going 69-93 in 2000, the Twins averaged 88 victories a year from 2001–08 and posted a winning record in seven of those eight seasons.

Smith credits Manager Ron Gardenhire — who took the reins in 2002 and led his squad to division titles in four of his first five seasons — and his coaches for creating an environment that allows young players to thrive. But the players are also quick to buy into the program and understand the value of certain organizational precepts. When homegrown products Joe Mauer, Justin Morneau and Michael Cuddyer reached the Major Leagues, it once again proved that the Twins were here to win.

Colorado rode a historic hot streak at the end of the 2007 season and stayed strong through sweeps of the Phillies and Diamondbacks in the NLDS and NLCS, respectively.

"The players come up through the system knowing each other, and there's always some camaraderie," Smith said. "Everybody pulls for each other, and by the time they get here, their wives and girlfriends all know each other. I think that's a huge plus."

SOARING TO THE TOP

Tony La Russa and Dave Duncan earned a reputation for sustained excellence as a manager-pitching coach tandem in Chicago, Oakland and St. Louis. But their performance with the 2006 Cardinals was impressive even by their own exacting standards.

Conventional wisdom holds that teams playing winning baseball late in the regular season are the best equipped to make a deep October run. So columnists were at a loss when trying to explain how the '06 Cards — who posted a 41-52 record after mid-June — limped into the playoffs as an 83-78 afterthought, and then blitzed San Diego in the NLDS and outlasted the New York Mets in the NLCS before eliminating the heavily-favored Detroit Tigers in the World Series.

The Cardinals won behind a reinvigorated Jeff Weaver, who was traded from Anaheim in July and pitched brilliantly in October. Albert Pujols hit .331 with 49 homers and 137 RBI to finish second in voting for the NL MVP Award, and David Eckstein batted .364 against Detroit to win the World Series MVP Award. As the Cardinals celebrated the franchise's 10th title in the clubhouse at the new Busch Stadium, they didn't seem to care how the outside world perceived them.

"A lot of people said we backed into the playoffs, and I have no resentment to that," said third baseman Scott Rolen. "But we didn't have to prove anything to anybody. We barely made the playoffs, and we turned around and played as good a caliber of baseball as we could play, and ended up being the world champions."

DOWN TO THE WIRE

Not only was the 2006 NLCS tied at three games apiece, but Game 7 at Shea Stadium was also tied, 1-1, heading into the ninth. The duel between the Mets and the Cardinals was a battle down to the very last out.

Mets left fielder Endy Chavez had robbed Scott Rolen of a two-run homer in the sixth, doubling Cardinals center fielder Jim Edmonds off first in the process. But Yadier Molina, just a .216 hitter with six home runs in the regular season, stepped to the plate with one man on in the ninth and delivered a blast to left that was too far gone for another theft from Chavez.

The Mets didn't go down without a fight, though, loading the bases in the bottom of the ninth. With two outs, however, Carlos Beltran looked at a called third strike on an Adam Wainwright curveball to give St. Louis its 17th NL pennant.

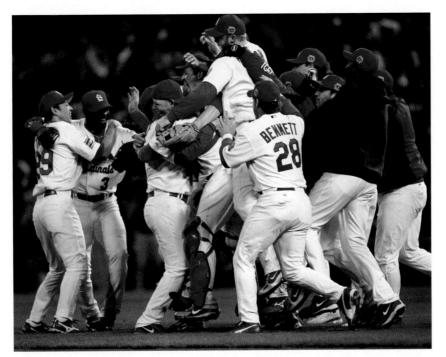

Opposite: Minnesota skipper Gardenhire before the 2004 Division Series at Yankee Stadium. This page: The Cardinals celebrate winning the 2006 World Series over the Tigers at Busch Stadium.

CHAPTER 11

CONFRONTATIONS

A classic confrontation can finish with an explosion — in the form of an Albert Pujols homer off Brad Lidge that nearly leaves the city of Houston proper — or as innocuously as the Yankees' Paul O'Neill jogging to first base after drawing a 10-pitch walk against Armando Benitez in the 2000 Subway Series. It can manifest itself as a shocking ninth-inning comeback against the most dominant closer ever, or in an impromptu smackdown between Pedro Martinez and Don Zimmer. Whatever they are or whomever they're between, this decade surely saw some good ones.

MOON SHOT

St. Louis first baseman Albert Pujols has a flair for baffling pitchers and making the opposing managers sweat. One of baseball's most feared sluggers, he also inspires confidence in his own teammates and keeps Cardinals fans expecting a key play when his team needs it most. During the 2005 National League Championship Series, he displayed his rare ability to wring joy from despair and turn a celebratory atmosphere into one marked by stone-cold silence.

The Cardinals — trailing the Astros, 3 games to 1, in the NLCS — were down to their final at-bat in Game 5 in Houston. Astros Manager Phil Garner called upon All-Star closer Brad Lidge, one of the game's shutdown relievers, who had notched 42 saves and averaged 13.1 strikeouts per nine innings pitched during the regular season.

But this save opportunity would be anything but routine. With two men out, David Eckstein grounded a single to left field and Jim Edmonds kept the rally going with a walk. More important, they both kept the inning alive so that Pujols could have a chance to extend the series with one swing.

Pujols took an awkward hack at a Lidge slider to begin his at-bat. But a second slider didn't surprise him, and Pujols didn't miss it. He drove the ball over the train tracks above the left-field wall at Minute Maid Park, and the ball smashed off the glass next to a bank of light towers. When Cardinals closer Jason Isringhausen retired the side in the bottom of the ninth, the stunned Astros suddenly realized the series was heading back to St. Louis.

"I've never heard 43,000 people shut up, just like that, in my life," said Cardinals outfielder Larry Walker. "One second you could barely hear in here. And the next second all that noise was gone. And the only noise you could hear was on our bench."

Despite losing the 2005 NLCS, Pujols had the most memorable moment of the series when, in Game 5 at Houston, he launched a Lidge offering over the left-field seats at Minute Maid Park. The ball still might not have landed.

Although the Astros won the next game to eliminate the Cardinals and move on to their first Fall Classic in franchise history, the home run became an emotional albatross for Lidge. He lost two games in the World Series against the White Sox — who ultimately swept the Astros — and was still being asked about his encounter with Pujols when he reported to Spring Training the next February.

"It doesn't deserve a lot of analysis," Lidge said. "I hung a slider, and he's Albert Pujols. I knew it was a bad pitch. The second it left my hand I knew he was going to kill it. When he hit it, my heart sank."

BEATING THE UNBEATABLE

THE SECRET TO success against Mariano Rivera, it appears, is keeping expectations to a minimum. That's a prudent strategy given the long line of hitters that the Yankees closer has abused and demoralized throughout his lengthy career.

When Arizona outfielder Luis Gonzalez stepped to the plate against Rivera in the ninth inning of Game 7 in the 2001 World Series, the scouting reports, the situation and a little voice in his head told him to concentrate on simply making contact and not worry about hitting the ball with authority.

"That's the first time I choked up all year," said Gonzalez, who slammed a career-high 57 home runs that season. "I knew the infield was playing in and I didn't have to try to hit it hard. I just had to loop something out there."

With the possible exception of Mookie Wilson's ground ball that went through Bill Buckner's legs in the 1986 World Series, never has a ball struck so softly endeared one man to so many fans. When Gonzalez dunked a bases-loaded flare over the head of short-stop Derek Jeter — who had won a World Series ring each of the previous four times he got there — to score Jay Bell and give the D-backs a 3-2 victory for the team's first world championship, it set off a wild celebration in Phoenix and assured that Gonzalez would never again have to pay for a meal in the city.

The victory also allowed the Diamondbacks to avoid a winter of "what ifs." Their closer, Byung-Hyun Kim, had blown ninth-inning leads in two excruciating losses at Yankee Stadium earlier in the Series.

"They got our ace twice in New York," Gonzalez said. "We got theirs once when it counted. I guess you can say it's even."

INSTANT CLASSIC

The 2001 World Series was a dramatic contest between seemingly mismatched combatants. In just their fourth year of existence, the underdog Arizona Diamondbacks held the New York Yankees, who were vying for their fourth straight world title, to just one run in the first two games of the Series. Arizona won both contests at home in Bank One Ballpark behind veterans Curt Schilling and Randy Johnson, who would each pitch in three games.

When the Series switched to the Bronx, the D-backs were unable to overcome New York's emotional post-Sept. 11 crowd. The Yankees dramatically swept the three games at Yankee Stadium, with Derek Jeter earning the title "Mr. November" for his walk-off homer in Game 4. The next night, Alfonso Soriano hit a walk-off single in the 12th inning of Game 5.

After a blowout win in Game 6, the fledgling Diamondbacks franchise became world champions in dramatic fashion on Nov. 4, coming from behind to win Game 7 on clutch hits from Tony Womack and Luis Gonzalez in the bottom of the ninth.

Teammates swarm Gonzalez (second from left) after he delivered an improbable bloop single against Rivera, the best postseason closer of all time, in a do-or-die Fall Classic showdown.

WALK THIS WAY

PAUL O'NEILL MADE his mark in New York for nine years with doubles to the gap, leaping catches at the fence and full-scale assaults on Gatorade buckets in the dugout. But perhaps his most memorable contribution in a Yankees uniform culminated in a jog to first base. O'Neill hit .474 for the Yankees in the 2000 World Series, but many observers pointed to his Game 1 walk against Mets closer Armando Benitez as the plate appearance that jump-started the Yankees to their fourth title in five seasons.

The Bronx Bombers trailed the Mets, 3-2, with one out in the ninth inning of the Series opener when O'Neill dug deep, relying on poise rather than his trademark passion. Af falling behind in the count, 1-2, against the hard-throwing Benitez, O'Neill fouled off two pitches, worked the count fu then fouled off two more before drawing a walk.

The momentum indisputably shifted to the Yankees in the course of those 10 pitches, and O'Neill's teammates made su to capitalize on his effort. Luis Polonia and Jose Vizcaino both singled to load the bases, and Chuck Knoblauch delivered a sa rifice fly to score O'Neill and tie the game, 3-3. The Yankees went on to win the opener, 4-3, on Vizcaino's bases-loaded sing in the 12th inning, and eliminated the Mets in five tightly contested games. And to think it all began with a test of wills.

"That was an unbelievable at-bat," said Manager Joe Torre. "You could tell that he made up his mind that he was going to give up the at-bat. It was sensational."

COMING OF AGE

WITH THE ACCESS he gained through his Hall-of-Fame father, Tony Gwynn Jr. enjoyed some notable perks as a Lit Leaguer, including an opportunity to pal around with the ballplayer who would eventually become one of the mc

> "YOU COULD TEL THAT O'NEILL MAD: UP HIS MIND THA' HE WASN'T GOING TC GIVE UP THE AT-BAT.
>
> JOE TORR

This page: Gwynn succeeded against San Diego's Hoffman in a crucial late-2007 game. Opposite: O'Neill's inspiring at-bat, and eventual run, against Benitez in Game 1 of the 2000 Subway Series turned the complexion of the game, and the Series, in the Yankees' favor.

prolific closers in baseball history. Gwynn Jr. was just 10 years old in 1993 when he struck up a friendship with the 26-year-old San Diego Padres closer Trevor Hoffman, and they spent many summer days talking baseball and throwing around a football in the outfield beneath the California sun.

Who could have envisioned that they would meet one day in a Major League game with so much on the line?

Hoffman and the Padres were on the verge of wrapping up an NL Wild Card berth on the final weekend of the 2007 season, but first they had to get past the Milwaukee Brewers — and an old acquaintance. It was not to be.

With San Diego clinging to a 3-2 lead in the ninth, Hoffman seemingly had Gwynn right where he wanted him with a 2-2 count. But Gwynn lined the next pitch to deep right field, delivering a game-tying triple off Hoffman. Milwaukee went on to win, 4-3, in 11 innings, leaving the Padres out of the playoff dance. Although many observers pointed to the irony in the match-up, Hoffman spent the winter carrying around a crushing emotional burden.

"I know it makes such a neat story," Hoffman said. "I just wish I hadn't come out on the wrong end of it. If he could have just had a 20-pitch at-bat and made an out, it would have been just as fun, don't you think?"

HOMEFIELD HEIST

In 2003, MLB raised the stakes for the All-Star Game, giving home-field advantage in the World Series to the winning league. The change was made in the aftermath of the 2002 contest that ended in a tie, and was also designed to address the trend of players declining to appear or leaving in the middle of the game.

At the 2006 Midsummer Classic in Pittsburgh, the importance of the game gave San Diego closer Trevor Hoffman just a little more reason to lament throwing the wrong pitch to Michael Young in the top of the ninth. During the previous day's media session, Hoffman made it clear that he relished the possibility of coming on in the ninth and trying to end the AL's nine-year unbeaten streak. When the NL carried a 2-1 lead into the top of the ninth, he got his wish.

But Hoffman didn't envision the struggle that followed. After recording two quick outs on comebackers by Jermaine Dye and Miguel Tejada, Hoffman surrendered a single to Paul Konerko and a ground-rule double to Troy Glaus.

With Hoffman ahead of Young, no balls and two strikes, he and catcher Brian McCann noticed Young creeping up in the batter's box in anticipation of the change-up, and they thought they could sneak a heater past him. The fastball came in at a lukewarm 86 mph, and Young lined it to right-center field to give the American League a lead it would not relinquish. When Yankees closer Mariano Rivera came on to record the save in the bottom of the ninth, it was another gut-wrenching loss for the NL.

"That's something that I am going to contemplate a few times," Hoffman said. "In most cases, I throw a change-up there. I probably should have gone with my bread and butter. To be that close, it hurts."

BLALOCK'S HEROICS

Before Michael Young's All-Star Game–winning at-bats in 2006 and 2008, it was teammate Hank Blalock who found himself at the plate in the eighth inning in 2003, facing the Dodgers' Eric Gagne with the AL down a run and a chance to take the lead.

The first-time All-Star knew that his teammates were depending on him. But that year, the game wasn't the only thing on the line. The 2003 All-Star Game marked the first time that the outcome "counted" — awarding the winning league home-field rights in the World Series — and the Rangers' third baseman wasn't about to let Gagne and the NL take the prize.

With two outs and a runner on second, Blalock certainly made his pinch-hit at-bat count. He launched the fourth pitch he saw as an All-Star over the right-center-field fence to give the Junior Circuit a 7-6 lead and eventual win, and ultimately give the Yankees home field in the Fall Classic.

At the 2006 All-Star Game, the AL earned World Series home-field advantage when Young drove a Hoffman pitch to the gap.

SHOWDOWN IN BEANTOWN

IN A DECADES-LONG rivalry that has produced countless tense moments and hard feelings, the Boston Red Sox and New York Yankees managed to add a new element to the equation in Game 3 of the 2003 American League Championship Series: They had their first intra-generational smackdown.

After Boston's Pedro Martinez threw a pitch over the head of Yankees outfielder Karim Garcia in the fourth — Garcia's first at-bat since an RBI single in the second inning — the reservoir of hostility reached a boil. Garcia got some retaliation that inning when he steamrolled Red Sox second baseman Todd Walker with a hard takeout slide. Then the benches emptied in the bottom of the frame when Red Sox left fielder Manny Ramirez took offense to a fastball up in the zone from Yankees starting pitcher Roger Clemens.

A garden-variety bench clearing became something more when Don Zimmer, the Yankees' 72-year-old bench coach, made a straight line for Martinez. The Boston pitcher, clearly caught off guard, grabbed Zimmer by the head and flung him to the ground.

There was plenty of contrition to go around after the game.

"I could never hit him. I would never do it," Martinez said. "I was just trying to dodge him and push him away, and too bad his body fell. I hope he's fine."

Zimmer, who was taken to the hospital as a precautionary measure, escaped with a pulled muscle and a minor cut on his head. During an emotional press conference the following day, he assailed Martinez for his lack of professionalism, but also seemed embarrassed by his role in the brawl.

"I'm retiring from fighting," Zimmer said. "I know now I'm way too old for this."

FAR EAST FACE-OFF

BASEBALL FANS AT Fenway Park looked on with curiosity as Boston's Daisuke Matsuzaka and Seattle's Ichiro Suzuki prepared to face off in April 2007. But the interest level in Boston and around the country didn't come close to the fervor in Japan, where the encounter transcended sports and attained the status of a cultural mega-event.

There was a history between the two, going back to 1999 in their homeland. Matsuzaka, a skinny, 18-year-old kid barely out of high school, struck out the 25-year-old Ichiro in three consecutive plate appearances. He would make nine more starts for Seibu against Ichiro's Orix team over two seasons, holding Ichiro to a cumulative .235 batting average on eight hits in 34 at-bats. In an interview with the *Seattle Times* just before the rematch with his countryman known as Dice-K, Ichiro sounded like a man yearning for redemption.

"I hope he arouses the fire that's dormant in the innermost recesses of my soul," said Ichiro, in a quote for the ages. "I plan to face him with the zeal of a challenger."

Major League Baseball estimated that an audience of about 20 million people would watch the rematch in Japan, even though the first pitch was scheduled for 8 a.m. local time. More than 100 Japanese media members were on hand, and they were covering the Dice-K vs. Ichiro matchup in as much detail as they did Japan's victory over Cuba in the 2006 World Baseball Classic.

Matsuzaka, in just his second start with the Red Sox, proved to be just as dominant against his old foe in the Major Leagues as he was in Japan, retiring Ichiro on a comebacker in the first inning, a flyout in the third, a strikeout in the fifth and a fielder's choice in the seventh. But both players were forced to take a backseat to Seattle starter Felix Hernandez, who carried a no-hitter into the eighth inning before allowing a single to J.D. Drew in a 3-0 Mariners victory.

Opposite: Yankees players and staff help Zimmer recover after being thrown down during a scuffle in Game 3 of the 2003 ALCS in Boston. Next spread: Matsuzaka rekindled a rivalry with fellow import, Ichiro, upon his arrival in the Majors.

CHAPTER 12

GLOBALIZATION

Baseball is still known as America's pastime, but the game expanded its reach in the 2000s. The influx of Latino talent, so impactful since the days of Roberto Clemente, continued with the arrival of new Latin American stars. Albert Pujols, Johan Santana and Miguel Cabrera were among the most prominent. Ichiro Suzuki helped to blaze a trail for Japanese players, and Team Japan won back-to-back titles in the World Baseball Classic. How soon before we see a large influx of Major Leaguers from China, Europe and other far-flung locales? Not as long as you might think.

INTERNATIONAL PASTIME

MAJOR LEAGUE BASEBALL's efforts to expand its global reach came into sharp focus at the 2005 winter meetings in Dallas, where the Commissioner's Office and the Players Association unveiled the particulars of the first World Baseball Classic, to be played in 2006.

The 16-team tournament was designed in part to extend the game's popularity beyond the traditional hotbeds of North America, Latin America and the Far East. The goal was to attract new audiences in areas such as Europe, Africa and China.

"I think this is going to take the whole international level of our sport to heights that we can't even imagine today," said Commissioner Bud Selig. "And while the World Series to me will always be the World Series, we're moving into a new era. There's no question about that."

With players from all 30 Big League clubs — including stars like Derek Jeter, Ichiro Suzuki and Justin Morneau — representing their homelands, the 2006 tournament was a big hit in several markets. Fans in Venezuela and the Dominican Republic quickly warmed to the concept, and Hiram Bithorn Stadium in San Juan was filled with raucous crowds for early-round games involving Puerto Rico.

The first Classic title went to Japan, which beat Cuba, 10-6, in the finale at San Diego's Petco Park. After Kosuke Fukudome's pinch-hit home run helped Japan beat South Korea, 6-0, in the semifinals, Mariners star Ichiro doubled, singled, drove in a run and scored three times against Cuba in the final. Ichiro, catcher Kenji Johjima and pitcher Akinori Otsuka were the only Major Leaguers on the Japanese roster, while Cuba had none.

Japan came back to defend its title in 2009, beating South Korea in the championship game at Dodger Stadium after eliminating the United States in the semifinals. Ichiro again

Members of Team Japan celebrate after defeating Team Cuba to win the inaugural World Baseball Classic in 2006.

played a leading role, delivering a two-run single in the 10th inning to give the Japanese squad a 5-3 victory.

"I believe that Ichiro's hit is something I'll never forget," said Japanese Manager Tatsunori Hara. "It's an image that will forever be imprinted in my mind."

By all substantive measures, the Classic achieved its goal of spreading the baseball gospel throughout the world. The number of sponsors grew from 26 in the first classic to 56 in the second. Tournament attendance increased from 737,112 to 801,408, and viewership for the nine games televised by ESPN increased 14 percent.

MADE IN JAPAN

MASANORI MURAKAMI BROKE new ground when he came to the United States in 1964 to pitch for the San Francisco Giants. It took 37 more years for the first Japanese position player — Ichiro Suzuki, eventually known simply as "Ichiro" — to sign with a Major League organization.

Ichiro arrived in Seattle in 2001, already with seven career batting titles, seven Gold Glove Awards and no shortage of expectations. Bobby Valentine, manager of the Chibe Lotte Marines in Japan and a former Major League skipper, called him one of the five best players in the world. And Ted Heid, the Mariners' director of Pacific Rim scouting, compared Ichiro's star power in Japan to Michael Jordan's appeal in the U.S.

"He's like Lewis and Clark," said Seattle Manager Lou Piniella. "I don't think he knows who Lewis and Clark were, though."

With an expansive Japanese press corps chronicling his every move, Ichiro lived up to the billing. He hit .350 and stole 56 bases in his first year with the Mariners, joining former Boston outfielder Fred Lynn as one of two players to win an MVP and Rookie of the Year Award in the same season.

Over the next four years, Hideki and Kazuo Matsui, Tadahito Iguchi, Kosuke Fukudome and other prominent Japanese position players left their homeland for the U.S., and Ichiro's status as a groundbreaker was assured. But he wasn't anywhere close to passing the torch: In 2008, Ichiro joined Wee Willie Keeler as the second player in history to post eight straight 200-hit seasons.

HAVE GLOVE, WILL TRAVEL

TORONTO FIRST BASEMAN Carlos Delgado knew something was different when he woke up the morning of the 2001 season opener and ate breakfast with his parents in San Juan, Puerto Rico. In hindsight, it was only the second most poignant moment of Delgado's day. The highlight came that night at Hiram Bithorn Stadium, when Texas Rangers catcher Ivan Rodriguez and outfielder Ricky Ledee ran from the dugout to the third-base line waving Puerto Rican flags in front of a capacity crowd.

"To come to the stadium and see it sold out, I got goosebumps during the introductions," Delgado said.

After opening the previous two seasons in Mexico and Japan, Major League Baseball came to Puerto Rico in an effort to revive the game on the island. Toronto's 8-1 victory over the Rangers lacked any semblance of drama or suspense, but it hardly mattered to the locals. A crowd of 19,891 sat at rapt attention before the game, when Hall of Famer Orlando Cepeda and Roberto Clemente's widow, Vera, threw out the ceremonial first pitches.

In the bleachers and at the concession stands, two cultures amicably collided. While fans drank pina coladas and ate pinchos, or chicken kebabs, the public address system

played rock music. The crowd even performed the wave at regular intervals. The fans generated an enthusiasm that resonated beyond gate receipts and the final score.

"I know I went 0 for 4 today, but I'm the happiest I've ever been," Rodriguez said.

LATIN INFLUENCE

DAVID ORTIZ WAS an 11-year-old boy in Santo Domingo when his father, for reasons unbeknownst to him, decreed that he should watch baseball on television and study the Twins in particular. Young David soon embraced center fielder Kirby Puckett as his role model, and eventually wore No. 34 in tribute.

"When I saw him go over the fence in the '91 World Series, he became my favorite player," Ortiz said.

In the 2000s, youthful Dominican dreamers still followed the game religiously on television. But they didn't have to look beyond their own front yard for inspiration. Major League Baseball perpetuated its tradition of developing great Latino players in the new millennium. About 25 percent of the players on Opening [D] rosters in 2005 came from Latin American countries — almost double the 13 percent in 1990.

Nowhere was the Latin influence more profound than at the 2005 All-Star Game in Detroit, where eight of the starting position players hailed from the Dominican Republic, Puerto Rico and Venezuela, and a ninth, New York Ci[ty] born Alex Rodriguez, was of Dominican descent. In addition, Venezuelan Bobby Abreu won the Home Run Derby as [his] young countryman, Miguel Cabrera, waved the nation's flag in tribute.

Dominicans Albert Pujols, Vladimir Guerrero, Miguel Tejada and Rodriguez all won MVP Awards in the decade, [and] Venezuela-born Johan Santana pocketed two Cy Young Awards. Meanwhile, a talented new wave led by phenoms such [as] Cabrera and Dominican Hanley Ramirez geared up to continue the legacy.

"A lot of young kids sitting at home in their countries see these guys who are hometown heroes, and it motivates the[m]," said long-time Major Leaguer Luis Gonzalez, who grew up in Florida after his parents fled Cuba in the late 1950s. "It g[ives] them hope they can make it to this level."

NORTH OF THE BORDER

GROWING UP IN Montreal in the early 1990s, Russell Martin would ride the subway to Olympic Stadium with his fat[her] to watch the Expos play. One of his favorite players was Larry Walker, a gifted right fielder and native Canadian, to bo[ot].

"He was amazing," Martin said. "Just the power to all fields, the consistency and the arm. He was a legit five-tool g[uy]. He was fun to watch."

In the 1990s, a young Canadian looking for a Big League role model could only choose between Walker and M[att] Stairs in the position-player ranks and Rheal Cormier and Denis Boucher among pitchers. Just over a decade la[ter], though, the opposite problem existed: An aspiring Canadian ballplayer barely knew where to begin. Hockey Cen[tral] became a baseball bastion in the 2000s. Justin Morneau won the 2006 American League Most Valuable Player Awa[rd] for the Minnesota Twins. Joey Votto made waves in Cincinnati with the Reds. Jason Bay became a fixture with [the] Pittsburgh Pirates and then the Boston Red Sox, and Martin emerged as one of the game's top catchers as a Los Ange[les] Dodger. The new wave of pitching was equally impressive. It included such names as Eric Gagne, Ryan Dempster, R[ich] Harden, Erik Bedard and Jeff Francis. At the 2008 All-Star Game at Yankee Stadium, Dempster, Morneau and Mar[tin] enjoyed the honor of representing Canada.

Abreu (center) and Cabrera proudly display their Venezuelan heritage at the Home Run Derby in 2005.

"There's a small percentage in the league, so to see three of that small percentage make the All-Star team is a lot of fun," Dempster said. "It's nice that we can go out there and laugh and all speak 'Canadian' to each other out on the field."

ISLAND SON

A GLANCE AT Major League Baseball's 2009 Opening Day rosters revealed that 229 players, or 28 percent, came from outside the United States. The talent pipeline spanned 15 countries and territories, ranging from old staples (the Dominican Republic, Venezuela and Puerto Rico) to some new and intriguing venues.

The Seattle Mariners had the most foreign-born players on an Opening Day roster with 15, while Atlanta won the award for geographic diversity. The Braves' representation spanned nine locations: the United States, Australia, Cuba, Curacao, the Dominican Republic, Japan, Mexico, Puerto Rico and Venezuela.

Curacao native Jair Jurrjens brings new meaning to the word "diverse." Jurrjens throws four quality pitches — two-seam and four-seam fastballs, a change-up and a slurve — and also speaks four languages. His linguistic repertoire consists of English, Spanish, Dutch and his native Papiamentu.

When Jurrjens won 13 games for Atlanta Braves and finished third in the 2008 Rookie of the Year balloting, his success was duly noted by the 140,000 residents of his native island off the coast of Venezuela. Several years ago, when Curacao sent a team to the Little League World Series, most of the youngsters identified Braves outfielder and fellow Curacao native Andruw Jones as their favorite player. Now their resident hero is Jurrjens, who made a surprise visit to Williamsport, Pa., to support the Curacao club in August 2008.

"He loves the game," explained Jurrjens' father, Carl. "This was always his dream, and now he's living it."

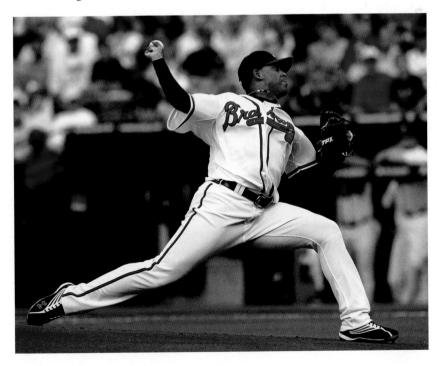

Opposite: Martin and Team Canada celebrate in the dugout after scoring a run against Team USA in the first round of the 2009 Classic. This page: Jurrjens had a breakout rookie year in 2008 and quickly became a hero on the island of Curacao.

147

CHAPTER 13
INSPIRATION

More than any sport, baseball provides an opportunity for athletes of average dimensions to accomplish extraordinary things. That sense of equality is reflected in diminutive David Eckstein's integral role on two world championship teams, and in soft-tossing left-hander Jamie Moyer fooling hitters long enough to win 250 games. Aside from giving hope to those of small stature, baseball has shown the power of redemption. No one embodies the "comeback" more than Josh Hamilton, a fallen prodigy who found a second chance in Cincinnati and Texas through baseball and his faith. Hamilton's hard-won baseball resurrection brought tears to the eyes of many. There's got to be a movie script here somewhere.

HAPPY ENDING

JON LESTER SPENT the winter of 2006–07 concentrating on things more important than perfecting his slider and working on his pitch location. A few months after doctors diagnosed him with anaplastic large cell lymphoma, Lester returned home to Tacoma, Wash., and endured a rigorous schedule of chemotherapy. Days and weeks that otherwise would have been devoted to preparing for Spring Training were filled with physical stress and emotional fallout from his battle with cancer.

So it seemed inspirational, in a fairy tale sort of way, that Lester would take the mound in October 2007 with the Boston Red Sox poised to clinch a World Series championship. At age 23, he had survived a bout with cancer and had become a walking endorsement for the power of happy endings. After Lester threw 5.2 innings to beat the Colorado Rockies, 4-3, and give Boston its second title in four years, his fellow Red Sox struggled to put the accomplishment into words.

"This is something you could make a movie about, when you think about all the challenges he has faced on a personal level and how much he has persevered," said Boston pitching coach John Farrell.

After hugging his parents and looking in vain for a trophy to embrace, Lester finally located that wonderful piece of hardware on the field beside the third-base dugout. He raised it joyfully over his head as the Boston fans in the box seats at Coors Field broke out into cheers.

"I don't think anybody in my position would have done anything different," Lester said. "That being said, if I can help out one person who's down in the dumps because they have cancer and it's not going well, maybe they'll say, 'If he could do it, I can do it.'"

Lester celebrates with his father following the decisive Game 4 of the 2007 World Series, less than a year after recovering from cancer.

But Lester wasn't content with a single moment of glory in October being his lone career highlight. On May 19, 2008, at Fenway Park — in the midst of a season in which he would finish with a 3.21 ERA and lead the Red Sox in innings pitched with 210.1 — he topped his exceptional World Series performance with a no-hitter in a 7-0 victory over Kansas City. It was the first no-hitter tossed by a Red Sox lefty since Mel Parnell did it in 1956. After the final out, Manager Terry Francona came onto the field and practically hugged the breath out of him.

"He said he was proud of me," Lester said. "We've been through a lot the last couple of years, and he has been like a second dad to me. It's just a special moment right there."

We might as well get used to it; the indomitable young left-hander has a lot of special moments in his arsenal.

TOUGH AS NAILS

WHEN DAVID ECKSTEIN'S teammates see the 5-foot-nothing infielder grit his teeth and dig into the batter's box, foul off tough pitches, and then head out into the field and sacrifice his body for groundballs in the hole, they know how consumed he is with making sure his club wins. There's nothing particularly unassuming about that, although his physique could be misleading.

Eckstein, who stands 5-foot-6 and 165 pounds — and walked on to his college baseball team at the University of Florida in 1994 before proving he deserved a scholarship — enjoyed a memorable run in the 2000s. He helped the Angels and Cardinals go the distance for a world title, becoming just the fourth shortstop in history to bat leadoff for two World Series winners. He joined some good company with Phil Rizzuto, Bert Campaneris and Maury Wills also accomplishing the feat.

In 2006, Eckstein delivered eight hits in his last 11 at-bats and posted a .500 slugging percentage to win the World Series MVP Award and help St. Louis upset Detroit in five games. He received a bright yellow Corvette — the first new car he had owned in his life — and rave reviews from his peers.

"He never takes a play off," said St. Louis infielder Aaron Miles. "He never takes an inning off. Make up a number — he goes 150 percent all the time."

Cardinals Manager Tony La Russa was equally impressed. He called Eckstein "the toughest guy I've ever seen in uniform" during the team's World Series run.

SEASONED VETERAN

JULIO FRANCO CALLED it "the hardest decision of my life" when he announced his retirement from baseball in May 2008. He was playing for the Quintana Roo Tigers in the Mexican League when, at age 49, he called it quits. In light of Franco's fanatical workout regimen and passion for the game, some of his contemporaries wondered if the day would ever come.

Franco left an indelible mark on baseball in his 31 professional seasons. He played for eight franchises, batted .298 for his career and accumulated 2,586 hits. Franco broke into the Big Leagues with a 1982 Phillies team that included future Hall of Famers Steve Carlton and Mike Schmidt, and played on a 2007 Mets team with All-Stars David Wright and Jose Reyes, neither of whom was even alive when Franco was a rookie.

Near the end, the Methuselah of the Big Leagues established several records for longevity. At age 48, he became the oldest player to hit a home run — against 43-year-old Randy Johnson, no less. He is also the oldest player to hit a grand slam, the oldest to

St. Louis's Eckstein was the 2006 World Series MVP, and a member of the 2002 world champion Angels.

homer twice in a game, the oldest to launch a pinch-hit home run, and the oldest to steal two bases in the same game.

Upon retiring, he could sense that it was the right time to go.

"I always said that I would be the first one to know the exact moment," Franco said. "I think the numbers speak for themselves, the production speaks for itself, and this is the right moment."

HOMERING HURLER

THE CARDINALS' RICK Ankiel didn't exactly arrive on the scene subtly. When he struck out 222 batters in 161 innings as a Minor Leaguer, several scouts and reporters — unfairly in hindsight — compared the 18-year-old southpaw to Hall of Famer Sandy Koufax.

Watching Ankiel dominate the Majors upon being called up in 2000, New York Mets Manager Bobby Valentine called him the "Alex Rodriguez of the pitching mound."

So it qualified as a shock when Ankiel experienced a sudden control meltdown in Game 1 of the National League Division Series against Atlanta in 2000, especially after going 11-7 in the regular season. Before long, people were mentioning him in the same sentence with Steve Blass — a dominant pitcher for the Pirates from 1964–72 who inexplicably lost his control after the '72 season and retired in 1974.

During the years when Ankiel should have been honing his craft on the mound, he approached the job of pitching with a newfound sense of dread. Once one of the game's

most promising talents, Ankiel was living out one of its saddest stories. After several years of futility and Tommy John surgery on his left elbow, it became evident that his baseball career was history. Or was it?

In the spring of 2005, Ankiel — always a good hitter — began a long, improbable journey back to the Big Leagues, channeling his time, effort and considerable athletic ability into a comeback as an outfielder. The payoff came in August 2007, when Ankiel arrived from his Minor League apprenticeship and proceeded to launch a three-run homer off San Diego hurler Doug Brocail in his outfield debut. The Busch Stadium crowd erupted, and Tony La Russa, the traditionally stoic Cardinals manager, became misty-eyed during his post-game press conference. Syndicated columnist Charles Krauthammer referred to Ankiel's comeback as "the stuff of legend."

For those who invoked Roy Hobbs, there was a more appropriate comparison. In 2008, Ankiel became just the second player in history to hit 25 or more home runs after having started 25 or more games as a pitcher. The other player to achieve the feat? Babe Ruth.

"Rick is one of the best athletes in the history of the world," said Cardinals right-hander Adam Wainwright.

A SECOND WIND

Jack McKeon enjoyed numerous perks after managing the Florida Marlins to a World Series victory over the New York Yankees in 2003.

During what the 73-year-old dubbed his "Gramps Across America" tour, McKeon charmed a David Letterman audience, sat in the back seat of parade convertibles and was profiled in *Cigar Aficionado* magazine. He cracked one-liners and dispensed second-hand smoke while proving that it's never too late for a second wind.

But the most gratifying moments came when McKeon sorted through his mail and read letters from fellow AARP members who took pride in seeing one of their peers become a national sensation.

"People say to me, 'I'm so inspired, I'm going back to apply for a job. Seeing the energy you've put out there has made us realize we can't just sit back here in a rocking

Opposite: Ankiel made a 2007 comeback as an outfielder after losing his control on the mound. This page: McKeon led the 2003 Florida Marlins to an unlikely world championship.

chair and die,'" McKeon said. "When you receive those letters, you feel like just maybe the good Lord put me in this position to invigorate some other people to help them along the way."

After replacing Jeff Torborg as Marlins skipper in May 2003, McKeon brought a sense of purpose to a young club. He led the team to a 75-49 regular-season record the rest of the way, followed by postseason victories over the Giants, Cubs and Yankees, and continued to win over the guys in the clubhouse even as he consistently mangled his players' names.

Was the absent-minded professor routine an act?

"He's got a good sense of humor," said Florida pitcher Carl Pavano. "Maybe he's having fun and this is his little inside joke. I wouldn't put it past him."

ONE MORE CHANCE

JOSH HAMILTON WAS in the woods of his home state of North Carolina, helping his brother cut trees to earn extra spending money for Christmas shopping, when he received some startling news: The Chicago Cubs had selected him from the Tampa Bay roster in Major League Baseball's 2006 Rule 5 draft and traded him to Cincinnati.

An hour later, Hamilton was on a conference call with reporters, sharing his sense of joy over having received one more chance.

"I can't even describe it," Hamilton said. "It's a dream come true. When you look at where I've been for the last three or four years, I just feel so fortunate that somebody has that kind of faith in me."

Over a span of several turbulent years, Hamilton had regressed from can't-miss super prospect to a walking cautionary tale. After Tampa Bay chose him first overall in the 1999 draft, Hamilton fell in with the wrong crowd and began a downward spiral of drug and alcohol abuse. Eventually he appeared to reach the point of no return, and was considered to be essentially out of the game when he returned to North Carolina.

But his story took an uplifting turn in 2007 when he hit 19 home runs for the Cincinnati Reds to gain a foothold on a Big League job. The Reds traded Hamilton to the Texas Rangers prior to the 2008 season, and it was there that he blossomed into the star he was once expected to become. The pinnacle of his comeback story came at the 2008 Home Run Derby at Yankee Stadium in New York. On that night, in front of a stadium full of supporters and millions watching on television all around the world, Hamilton slugged a single-round record 28 home runs, including three that traveled farther than 500 feet. He soon shared his message of hope in a book, *Beyond Belief: Finding the Strength to Come Back.*

"Baseball is third in my life right now, behind my relationship with God and my family," Hamilton wrote. "Without the first two, baseball isn't even in the picture. Believe me, I know."

Hamilton recovered from drug and alcohol abuse to take his place as one of the best hitters in the Major Leagues.

"IT'S A DREAM COME TRUE. WHEN YOU LOOK AT WHERE I'VE BEEN FOR THE LAST THREE OR FOUR YEARS, I JUST FEEL SO FORTUNATE THAT SOMEBODY HAS THAT KIND OF FAITH IN ME." JOSH HAMILTON

BIBLIOGRAPHY

CHAPTER 1

9. "Schilling takes pride in 'hero' designation." Blum, Ronald. "Ol' blood and guts, Schilling stomps on Cardinals." Associated Press 25 Oct. 2004.

9. "Schilling's sock makes it to Cooperstown." Culpepper, Chuck. "Bloody sock is rocking the Hall." *Newsday* 13 April 2005: A67.

10. "Fan praises Rowand for toughness in letter to editor." Kozlowski, David E. "Aaron Rowand's the kind of guy you want in your foxhole." *Philadelphia Daily News* 17 May 2006: 18.

10. "Graffanino distracted by bird in no-hitter." Gage, Tom. "Brewers sensed trouble early; Verlander's speedy fastball, wicked breaking pitches and seagull pals made for a tough night." *The Detroit News* 13 June 2007: 4D.

11. "Moths bring gulls to Detroit." Mannix, Chris, and Epstein, Dave. "Comerica Park's Seagulls." *Sports Illustrated* 25 June 2007.

14. "J.T. Snow recounts his save of Baker's son at home plate." McCauley, Janie. "Manager's bat boy son escapes injury in close call at plate." Associated Press 25 Oct. 2002.

17. "Derek Jeter on his quick thinking to nail Giambi at the plate." Curry, Jack. "New Mr. October Polishes His Growing Luster, and Keeps Yankees Alive." *The New York Times* 14 Oct. 2001: Section 8: Page 3.

17. "Steinbrenner full of praise for Yankees' Jeter." Popper, Steve. "Add Catch To Jeter's Catalog Of Heroics." *The New York Times* 16 Oct. 2001: Section S; Page 3.

17. "Steve Bartman issues an apology." Mercury News wire services. "As Chicago vents, fan apologizes.' *San Jose Mercury News* 16 Oct. 2003: 1A.

17. "Bartman ball sold, then blown up." Davey, Monica. "Long-Suffering Cubs Fans Hope Blasted Ball Puts End to 'Curse.'" *The New York Times* 27 Feb. 2004: 16.

17. "Red Sox fans still grateful to Roberts for steal." Goldberg, Jeff. "Roberts draw fans' gratitude." *Hartford Courant* 16 June 2007: C5.

18. "Rockies' Holliday celebrates his winning slide." Moore, C.J. "Holliday plays like an MVP — as usual." MLB.com 2 Oct. 2007.

22. "Ernie Banks give pep talk at All-Star Game." Blum, Ronald. "Drew vs. Wright: The matchup that might have been." Associated Press 17 July 2008.

22. "Mariano Rivera and Michael Young react to the marathon finale at Yankee Stadium." Harrington, Mike. "New York marathon; Major League Baseball All-Star Game: Midsummer Classic turns into long day's night in Bronx." *Buffalo News* 16 July 2008: D1.

23. "Little reflects on his decision to leave Martinez in the game." Golen, Jimmy. "Red Sox won't have Little back; Gut decision in playoffs may have been a factor." Associated Press 28 Oct. 2003.

23. "The celebrities come out for first game back at Shea." Walker, Ben. "Piazza adds final touch Two-run homer caps emotional night at Shea." Associated Press 22 Sept. 2001.

23. "Piazza fought back tears." Lelinwalla, Mark. "Piazza's homer still remembered as a shot for the ages." New York *Daily News* 27 Sept. 2008.

23. "Glavine on the special feeling at Shea." DiComo, Anthony. "Piazza's post 9/11 HR helped heal city." MLB.com 7 Aug. 2007.

CHAPTER 2

27. "Dodgers celebrate with catered steak dinner." Gurnick, Ken. "Dodgers set modern record for home start: Seven-run outburst in sixth leads way to 13-0 mark in LA." Gurnick, Ken. MLB.com 7 May 2009.

27. "Joe Torre on the Dodgers' long-term goals." Associated Press. "Dodgers set ML record with 13-0 start at home." 7 May 2009.

27. "General Manager Ned Colletti on the Dodgers' fast start at home.'" Shaikin, Bill. "It isn't a title yet, but it's a nice start." *Los Angeles Times* 7 May 2009; Part C; Page 9.

28. "Omar Vizquel reacts to breaking Aparicio's record." McCauley, Janie. "Giants honor Omar Vizquel for most games at shortstop." Associated Press 31 May 2008.

31. "Atlanta General Manager John Schuerholz on the magnitude of the team's postseason streak." Odum, Charles. "Phillies-Braves rained out, Braves eliminated from NL East race." Associated Press 13 Sept. 2006.

31. "Derek Jeter expresses his disappointment over Yankees' failure to make the postseason." Feinsand, Mark. "No October For Yanks This Year." New York *Daily News* 24 Sept. 2008: 60.

31. "Jimmy Rollins and Chase Utley react differently to their streaks." Devaney Jr., Kevin. "Utley's streak no longer after 0-for-5 night." *Home News Tribune* 5 Aug. 2006.

32. "Ichiro breaks record to the accompaniment of fireworks." Andriesen, David. "Ichiro breaks 84-year-old record for hits in a season." *Seattle Post-Intelligencer* 2 Oct. 2004.

32. "Ichiro calls hits record the highlight of his career." Sherwin, Bob. "HITS-TORY! Ichiro breaks Sisler's record." *Seattle Times* 2 Oct. 2004.

33. "Baltimore's Kevin Millar reacts to Texas' 30-run outburst." Kubatko, Roch. "Drubbed: O's Allow Most Runs in Game Since 1900, Then Get Swept." *Baltimore Sun* 23 Aug. 2007.

33. "Texas outfielder Marlon Byrd on the Rangers' 30-run outburst." Ginsberg, David. "Thirty. That's Something. Rangers Set AL Record on Day Trembley Re-Ups." Associated Press 23 Aug. 2007.

35. "Billy Wagner and Joe Torre react to the Astros' no-hitter at Yankee Stadium." Blum, Ronald. "Record six Houston pitchers no-hit Yankees." Associated Press 12 June 2003.

35. "Carl Crawford unaware of his record-tying feat." Goodall, Fred. "Crawford swipes 6 bases in Rays win." Associated Press 4 May 2009.

36. "Craig Biggio on his inability to get out of the way of HBPs." Garber, Greg. "Plunk'd. The latest, greatest Craig Biggio story." ESPN.com. 17 July 2007.

36. "Ian Kinsler pays tribute to Jackie Robinson after going 6 for 6 with a cycle." Sullivan, T.R. "Speedster calls Robinson Day performance best of career." MLB.com 16 April 2009.

CHAPTER 3

37. "Jon Wehner reacts to PNC Park in Pittsburgh." Haudricourt, Tom. "New park restores life to Pittsburgh baseball; Stadium offers skyline view, hope for Pirates." *Milwaukee Journal Sentinel.* 20 May 2001: 8C.

37. "Grounds crew re-measures distance to outfield fences." Salisbury, Jim, and Zolecki, Todd. "Distance detectives get full measure of facts; Team opens its tapes to public and dimensions ring true." *Philadelphia Inquirer* 25 July 2004: D5.

37. "J.T. Snow reacts to Citizens Bank Park after first batting practice." Zolecki, Todd. "Phillies' new palace is no place for a pitcher." *Philadelphia Inquirer* 3 Oct. 2004: D7.

39. "Mike Lieberthal mesmerized by Phillies' new home." Salisbury, Jim. "Home Sweet Home; Phillies, still in awe over park, are ready to make history in it." *Philadelphia Inquirer* 3 April 2004: D1.

39. "Owner Peter Magowan praises Giants' new ballpark." Markiewicz, David A. "Back to the future; Latest wave of new ballparks tries to improve on retro trend of '90s." Fort Worth Star-Telegram 14 July 1999: 1.

39. "Chipper Jones talks about pitcher-friendly dimensions at Citi Field." Interview on "Ripken Baseball" on Sirius XM Baseball.

CHAPTER 4

53. "Manager Bob Melvin greets Webb after his streak ends." Boivin, Paola. "Streak Ends for Webb, But That's a Good Thing." *The Arizona Republic* 23 Aug. 2007: Sports, 1.

55. "Chris Snyder marvels at Webb's streak." Piecoro, Nick. "Done In One; Webb's Streak Ends." *The Arizona Republic.* 23 Aug. 2007.

55. "Peavy expresses support for Hoffman after blown save." Krasovic, Tom. "KKKKKKKKABLOOEY; Franchise record-tying 16 strikeouts by Peavy becomes a footnote as Drew's two-run homer in the bottom of the ninth gives Arizona a victory." *The San Diego Union-Tribune* 26 April 2007: D1.

58. "Cliff Lee elated over Cy Young selection." Hoynes, Paul. "Posed with poise: a winning routine." *Plain Dealer.* 14 Nov. 2008: D1.

59. "Arizona manager Bob Brenly reflects upon Johnson's perfect game." McManaman, Bob. "27 up … 27 down; Johnson, 40, oldest to toss perfect game." *The Arizona Republic.* 19 May 2004: 1C.

59. "Roger Clemens praises his Houston teammate, Roy Oswalt." De Jesus Ortiz, Jose, and McTaggart, Brian. "Affirmed Ace." *The Houston Chronicle* 1 April 2007: 8.

61. "Red Sox Manager Jimy Williams on Pedro Martinez's 2000 season." Dubow, Josh. "Martinez sweeps in Cy Young; Boston ace is first to win AL Award unanimously in consecutive seasons." Associated Press 14 Nov. 2000.

61. "Mets Manager Jerry Manuel raves about Santana's performance." Lennon, David. "METS 2, MARLINS 0: Johan gets win and save; Rescues season with three-hitter as Mets tie for wild-card lead." *Newsday* 28 Sept. 2008: B3.

CHAPTER 5

63. "Justin Morneau talks about Josh Hamilton's home run display." Bloom, Barry M. "Morneau stuns Hamilton to take Derby." MLB.com 14 July 2008.

64. "Hamilton homers on 13 straight swings." Stark, Jayson. "Hamilton's power display defies explanation." ESPN.com 14 July 2008.

64. "Hamilton recalls swinging in his backyard." Cothran, Jeremy. "Josh Hamilton is sleepy (and awesome)." *The Star-Ledger* 14 July 2008.

64. "Charlie Manuel on Ryan Howard." Dubois, Lou. "Phils Slugger Ryan Howard Lets His Bat Do His Talking, and So Far It Has Made Such a Ruckus." *Sports Illustrated Presents* 5 Nov. 2008: 62.

67. "Rodriguez hugs Abreu and Jeter at home plate." Hoch, Bryan. "A-Rod belts historic 500th homer." MLB.com 4 Aug. 2007.

67. "Aaron praises Fielder at awards ceremony." Bloom, Barry. "Rodriguez, Fielder earn Aaron Awards." MLB.com 28 Oct. 2007.

67. "Prince Fielder reacts to 50th home run." Jenkins, Chris. "Fielder reaches 50 HRs as Brewers power past Cardinals 9-1." Associated Press 26 Sept. 2007.

68. "Barry Bonds hugs son at home plate." Curry, Jack. "Bonds Completes a Rocky Journey." *The New York Times* 8 Aug. 2007.

68. "Hafner watched Don Mattingly on television as a youth." Associated Press. "N.D. native ties 'Donnie Baseball' slam record." 13 Aug. 2006.

69. "Jim Thome hoisted aloft by Dye and Jenks after 500th home run." Gano, Rick. "Thome's 500th homer gives White Sox 9-7 victory over Angels." Associated Press 17 Sept. 2007.

69. "Gary Sheffield reacts to his 500th career homer." Rumberg, Howie. "Sheffield hits 500th home run." Associated Press 18 April 2009.

73. "Vladimir Guerrero on his free-swinging approach." Saxon, Mark. "Vladimir Guerrero is one of baseball's most talented players — and its quietest." *Sports Illustrated* Aug. 2005: 24.·

73. "Tim Salmon compares Guerrero to Clemente." Modesti, Kevin. "Guerrero Has Us All Giddy." The *Daily News* of Los Angeles. 9 March 2004: S1.

74. "Griffey recalls his trip around the bases." Sheldon, Mark. "Griffey joins kings of clout with No. 600." MLB.com 10 June 2008.

74. "Griffey received calls from Mays and Aaron. Sheldon, Mark. "Griffey joins kings of clout with No. 600. MLB.com 10 June 2008.

CHAPTER 6

78. "Willis gets threatened with fine by Torborg for slide." Barnes, Craig. "Game of chances; after Mets sting, Stratton happy to have an opportunity with Marlin" *Sun-Sentinel* 10 March 2003: 11C.

78. "Poll names Casey baseball's friendliest player." SI.com. "Who is the friendliest player in baseball?" 16 May 2007.

80. "Ozzie Guillen talks about dying on the baseball field." Morrissey, Rick. "Ozzie Guillen shares his inimitable Ozzie Guillen philosophy on death." *Chicago Tribune* 26 Feb. 2009.

81. "Heath Bell and his fondness for toys." Wilson, Bernie. "Heath Bell to ring in new era for Padres." Associated Press 2 April 2009.

81. "Bell says he's a nice guy at heart." Kurkjian, Tim. "Fun-loving Bell finally has his dream job." *ESPN The Magazine* 17 April 2009.

81. "Eric Byrnes and his hairstyle." Reaves, Joseph A. "Byrnes nets 3-year, $30 mil deal." *The Arizona Republic* 8 Aug. 2007: 8.

81. "Byrnes invites Little Leaguers to his house." Bickley, Dan. "Gonzalez set to cheer for old team." *The Arizona Republic* 21 Sept. 2007.

85. "Ozzie Guillen on Pierzynski's lack of popularity." Souhan, Jim. "Pierzynski is Eddie Haskell in shin guards." *Star Tribune* 27 Aug. 2006.

85. "Mark Buehrle on the Pierzynski-Barrett confrontation." Keown, Tim. "White Noise: A.J. Pierzynski loves to win. He just has a funny way of showing it." *ESPN The Magazine* 21 Aug. 2006.

85. "Pierzynski responds to booing at wrestling event." Cowley, Joe. "Pierzynski: The man everyone loves to hate: White Sox catcher turns being bad guy into an art form." *Chicago Sun Times* 4 March 2007.

85. "David Wells and Charles Barkley exchange digs over their weight." Penner, Mike. "David Wells talks a good game on TBS." *The Los Angeles Times* 15 May 2009.

CHAPTER 7

87. "Morneau on Mauer's impact in the batting order." Miller, Phil. "Joe Mauer, Justin Morneau: M's of a feather for the Minnesota Twins." *St. Paul Pioneer Press* 22 May 2009.

89. "Gardenhire on the importance of Mauer and Morneau to the lineup." Neal III, La Velle E. "Joe Mauer and Justin Morneau hit consecutive homers for the second night in a row, and the Twins beat the Mariners again." *Star Tribune* 10 May 2009.

93. "Chipper Jones on his early switch-hitting goals." Rogers, Carroll. "BOTH SIDES WOW: How Chipper became this era's greatest switch hitter." *The Atlanta Journal-Constitution* 11 May 2008: 5E.

93. "Cal Ripken Jr. on Alex Rodriguez's All-Star Game tribute." Hawkins, Stephen. "A-Rod tribute to Ripken erases negatives." Associated Press 17 July 2001.

93. "Ripken made Schilling think of Ted Williams." Justice, Richard. "Curtain Cal;Ripken helps AL prevail by going out with a bang." *The Houston Chronicle* 11 July 2001: Sports, P.1.

93. "Mets GM Omar Minaya on the fans' connection to Wright and Reyes." Lennon, David. "Different strokes; Reyes, Wright may have opposite personalities and styles but they complement one another on the field." *Newsday* 26 Feb. 2006: B2.

96. "Wright shares his desire to be a mainstay in New

York." Vaccaro, Mike. "They're hard core — left-side stars ready to shoulder burden." The *New York Post* 19 Feb. 2009: 71.

96. "Diamondbacks GM Joe Garagiola Jr. on the Johnson-Schilling tandem." Dvorchak, Robert. "Johnson, Schilling: Arizona's mystique, aura." *Pittsburgh Post-Gazette* 6 Nov. 2001: D1.

99. "Atlanta General Manager John Schuerholz and pitcher John Smoltz recall the special synergy of the Big Three." Rogers, Carroll. "A mound of memories; 'Big Three': Glavine, Smoltz and Maddux will be back together again — sort of — at Turner Field." *The Atlanta Journal-Constitution* 6 May 2008: 1D.

99. "Yvonne Upton marvels over her sons' ability." Livingstone, Seth. "Uptons: Two sons, two stars; Mom, Dad two-fer (B.J., Justin) in raising major league talent." *USA Today* 25 March 2008: 1C.

99. "A.J. Hinch is high on Justin Upton's career prospects." Bordow, Scott. "D-Backs' Upton developing into a superstar." *East Valley Tribune* 27 May 2009.

CHAPTER 8

101. "McKeon explains his decision to pitch Beckett on short rest against Yankees." Botte, Peter. "It's sink or swim against Big Fish: Beckett to go on short rest." New York *Daily News* 25 Oct. 2003: 54.

101. "McKeon reacts to Beckett's performance." Sullivan, T.R. "Series: It's a fine kettle of Fish; Above the rest, Florida's Beckett caps Marlins' conquest of Yankees." *Fort Worth Star Telegram* 26 Oct. 2003: 1C.

103. "Beckett shares his post-World Series plans." Walker, Ben. "Incredible journey by Marlins: Gutted after title in '97, Florida returns to top with young arm, 72-year-old manager." Associated Press 27 Oct. 2003.

103. "Johnson says Lincecum looks like a Jonas brother." Nightengale, Bob. "Lincecum's special delivery; Giants' Cy Young winner has a baby face, a crazy motion and a killer fastball." *USA Today* 17 March 2009: 1C.

103. "Lincecum says he hasn't changed." Stone, Larry. "New challenges for Lincecum; The Cy Young Award winner must handle the accompanying hoopla with care." *The Seattle Times* 15 March 2009: D5.

103. "Zimmer compares Longoria to Schmidt and Robinson." Antonen, Mel. "Minor start, major player; Since his promotion, the Rays' Longoria has been a big hit." *USA Today* 6 Aug. 2008: 1C.

108. "Buddy Bell would start a team with Sizemore." Dutton, Bob. "Sizemore sets the ton for Indians." *The Kansas City Star* 13 Oct. 2007: D5.

108. "Baker's story about Ramirez's basketball prowess." Kurkjian, Tim. "Ramirez making the game look easy." ESPN.com 16 Feb. 2009.

108. "Marlins' Uggla praises his teammate, Ramirez." Kepner, Tyler. "A Star in the Making Takes His Place at the Top of the Order." *The New York Times* 15 July 2008.

108. "Ramirez ranks fifth in The Sporting News survey." Capozzi, Joe. "Hanley Ramirez ranks 5th best among current players." *Palm Beach Post* 20 May 2009.

108. "Hernandez was overwhelmed by the early buildup." Larue, Larry. "Finding Felix." *The Tacoma News Tribune* 25 March 2007: C1.

CHAPTER 9

111. "Maddux on Hoffman's 500th save." Krasovic, Tom. "Ring up No. 500; Hoffman raises his own career saves record to landmark level." *The San Diego Union-Tribune*. 7 June 2007: D-1.

113. "Tracy compares Gagne to DiMaggio and Ripken." Plunkett, Bill. "Gagne accepts inactivity; The lack of save chances doesn't bother him, he says, as long as the Dodgers win games." *The Orange County Register* 15 June 2004.

114. "Posada calls Rivera the best closer ever." O'Brien, Kat. "Mo, Trevor; Save memory." *Newsday* 20 June 2008: A72.

116. "Rodriguez feels grandfather's presence during record-setting moment." Baxter, Kevin. "58!; Rodriguez sets the Major League single-season record for saves in the Angels' 5-2 victory over Seattle." *Los Angeles Times* 14 Sept. 2008: D13.

116. "Lidge reflects on celebrating the final out of the World Series." Maadi, Rob. "Lidge has tough task following perfect season." Associated Press 20 Feb. 2009.

116. "Sutter cried when he got the Hall call." Ostermeier, Joe. "Pitcher makes it after 13-year wait." Belleville (Ill.) *News-Democrat* 11 Jan. 2006.

CHAPTER 10

120. "Mike Cameron reflects upon Seattle's 116-win season." Howard, Johnette. "Mariners Couldn't Stem the Inevitable." *Newsday* 24 Oct. 2001: A83.

120. "Billy Beane discusses the fallout from the *Moneyball* book." Shaughnessy, Dan. "Beane has looked sharp by doing things his way." *The Boston Globe* 28 Sept. 2003.

122. "Rockies' Helton proud of team's World Series appearance." Renck, Troy E. "Broomsday: Sox sweep Series. Rockies' miraculous late-season surge comes to a sad ending in final four games." *The Denver Post* 28 Oct. 2007.

125. "Scott Rolen talks about Cardinals' road to the World Series." Leach, Matthew. "Cards secure 10th World Series title: Proud franchise adds to long legacy of championship teams. 28 Oct. 2006.

CHAPTER 11

127. "Larry Walker's reaction to Albert Pujols' home run off Brad Lidge." Stark, Jayson. "How Pujols changed the world." ESPN.com 17 Oct. 2005.

128. "Brad Lidge reflects on Pujols' home run." Antonen, Mel. "Lidge keeps driving ahead." *USA Today* 16 Jan. 2006.

128. "Luis Gonzalez on his approach at the plate and the comeback from Byung-Hyun Kim's blown saves." Harrington, Mike. "Yankees Dynasty is Gonzo: Arizona Outfielder Lives Dream." *Buffalo News* 5 Nov. 2001.

130. "Torre on O'Neill's at-bat against Benitez." Curry, Jack. "Game Turns on a Pressure-Packed At-Bat." *The New York Times* 22 Oct. 2000: Section 8; 1.

133. "Hoffman reflects on Tony Gwynn Jr. at-bat." Nightengale, Bob. "Disappointment aside, Hoffman still stands tall." *USA Today* 3 March 2008.

133. "Trevor Hoffman on his approach against Michael Young in the All-Star Game." Troy E. Renck. "Ninth-inning rally lifts AL to victory: Young's two-out, two-run triple extends NL misery." *Denver Post*, Page D-1; 12 July 2006.

135. "Pedro Martinez describes his confrontation with Don Zimmer." Blum, Ronald. "Yankees 4, Red Sox 3." Associated Press. 12 Oct. 2003.

135. "Don Zimmer reacts to the confrontation with Martinez." Madden, Bill. "Aching Zim Rips Pedro But Regrets His Actions." New York *Daily News* 13 Oct. 2003: 59.

CHAPTER 12

139. "Bud Selig's vision for the WBC." Associated Press. "WBC teams rounding into shape." 6 Dec. 2005.

140. "Ichiro's hit leaves lasting impression on Manager Hara." Curry, Jack. "Ichiro Suzuki Delivers Memorable End to World Baseball Classic." *The New York Times* 24 March 2009.

140. "Summary of WBC success." Major League Baseball release. "World Baseball Classic Achieves Major Off-Field Successes; New Highs for Attendance, Ratings and Sponsorship Are Achieved." 25 March 2009.

140. "Valentine calls Ichiro one of world's five best players." Farber, Michael. "Rising Son; The defection of Ichiro Suzuki, a career .353 hitter, isn't seen as all bad news in Japan, if he becomes a sensation with the Mariners and brings honor to his country." *Sports Illustrated* 4 Dec. 2000: 68.

140. "Mariners' Heid compares Ichiro to Michael Jordan." Newhan, Ross. "Ichiro Suzuki (please, just call him Ichiro), is an icon in Japan, but he just wants to prove himself with the Mariners." *Los Angeles Times* 9 March 2001: 13.

140. "Lou Piniella compares Ichiro to Lewis and Clark." Hickey, John. "Ichiro's Impact is immediate; Japanese star makes smooth transition to major leagues." *The Seattle Post-Intelligencer* 30 March 2001: F4.

147. "MLB's geographic diversity." Major League Baseball release. "Opening Day rosters feature 230 players born outside the U.S." 6 April 2009.

147. "Carl Jurrjens on his son's love for baseball." Williams, Mike. "The home of Jair Jurrjens: Base island;

Baseball-crazy Curacao is mad about its latest native son to do it proud as an Atlanta Brave." *The Atlanta Journal-Constitution* 20 July 2008: 1D.

CHAPTER 13

150. "Francona shares his sense of pride with Lester." Horrigan, Jeff. "Lester to Royals: No way; Sox lefty unhittable at Fenway." *The Boston Herald* 20 May 2008:54.

150. "LaRussa praises Eckstein for his toughness." O'Brien, David. "Everything stacks for Cards; Eckstein, another late error bedevil Tigers in collapse." *The Atlanta Journal-Constitution* 27 Oct. 2006: 7E.

150. "Julio Franco on the difficulty of his retirement decision." Ocker, Sheldon. "More to the Julio Franco

story than just baseball." *Akron Beacon Journal* 10 May 2008.

152. "Franco on knowing the right time to go." Associated Press. "Franco finally calls it quits." 4 May 2008.

152. "Valentine compares Ankiel to Alex Rodriguez." Heyman, Jon. "Ankiel Must Stop His Walk on the Wild Side." *Newsday* 1 March 2002: A77.

153. "Ankiel's comeback is legendary." Krauthammer, Charles. "'The Natural' returns; Ankiel's redemption thrills, even as real world awaits." *Chicago Tribune*. 20 Aug. 2007: 19.

154. "Josh Hamilton on baseball's place in his life." Hamilton, Josh (as told to Tim Keown). "I'm proof that hope is never lost." *ESPN The Magazine*. 5 July 2007.

CREDITS

INDEX